HUMAN RESOURCES DEVELOPMENT

Intervention and Collaboration: Helping Organizations to Change

Intervention and Collaboration: Helping Organizations to Change

Hedley G. Dimock

Amsterdam • Johannesburg • London
San Diego • Sydney • Toronto

Copyright © 1975, 1976, 1981, 1992, 1993
by Hedley G. Dimock
Hardcover: ISBN 0-88390-361-X
Paperback: ISBN 0-88955-053-0
Library of Congress Catalog Card Number: 92-41683

Printed in the United States of America.

Library of Congress Cataloging-in-Publication Data
Dimock, Hedley G. (Hedley Gardner)
    Intervention and collaboration: helping organizations
to change/ Hedley G. Dimock.
        p.   cm.
    Includes bibliographical references.
    ISBN 0-88390-361-X
    1. Organizational change. 2. Corporate culture. 3. Group
relations training.   I. Title.
HD58.8.D56   1993
658.4'063—dc20   92-41683
                                                        CIP

Pfeiffer & Company
8517 Production Avenue
San Diego, California 92121-2280 USA
(619) 578-5900 FAX: (619) 578-2042

This book is printed on acid-free, recycled stock that
meets or exceeds the minimum GPO and EPA specifications
for recycled paper.

Table of Contents

Preface vii

PART ONE
The Intervention and Collaborative
Change Model 1

PART TWO
Personal Qualities of the Intervener-Consultant 9

PART THREE
Getting Ready for an Intervention 13
   Assumptions About Changing Social Systems . . . 20
   Starting an Intervention 30

PART FOUR
Outline for an Intervention 33
   Power Analysis 36

PART FIVE
Organizing an Intervention 41
   Entry 41
   Data Collection and Analysis 47
   Goal Setting 61
   Action Planning 65
   Action Taking 68
   Evaluation and Replanning 70
   Establishing Closure 71

PART SIX
Evaluating Interventions 75

PART SEVEN
Organizing and Leading Interventions 87

PART EIGHT
Personal Concerns of the Intervener 105

Bibliography 115

Resources 117
   Resource A: Organization-Scan Guide 119
   Resource B: Community-Scan Guide 123
   Resource C: The Ten Most Widely Used Aids to
      Decision Making 127
   Resource D: The Ten Best Ways to Improve Meeting
      Effectiveness 129
   Resource E: Checklist for Assessing an
      Intervention Plan 131

PREFACE

This book is for everyone who wants to change the way things get done in their groups, organizations, and communities. Although most people have ideas about what should be done to improve things, the potential readers of this book are those who are prepared to take some initiative and responsibility for implementing ideas for change. As such, these potential readers either will be people who want to make the programs with which they work more effective or they will be staff trainers and consultants who want to help others. Hopefully too, some of these will be social activists intent on humanizing the institutions that impact our lives.

The collaborative methods of planning new ways of doing things that are described here are immensely popular yet they are talked about far more than they are used. There are two reasons for this gap between policy and practice: (1) Interveners often are reluctant to share their power, and (2) collaborative projects frequently fail. Both issues are addressed in this book.

To begin, interveners/consultants are encouraged to be more open about their strengths and weaknesses in order to help trust themselves more and thus consider trusting others to make decisions. The Intervention and Collaborative Change method describes how this can be done safely and effectively.

Second, empowering others to take responsibility for themselves is challenging enough, but getting a fair number of these empowered people to cooperate on joint planning as equals is overwhelmingly difficult. Success requires a great deal of group skills from the intervener and these skills are not often taught in training programs or described in books. Change programs lacking the competence to make the planning group effective begin to flounder, go in circles, and generate frustration. Either the project collapses at this point or it is given to or taken over by a strong leader who repudiates the very collaborative planning that is part of the unique focus of this book.

In trying to help interveners through the procedures of effective collaborative planning, I sense that my presentation may seem like a how-to-do-it blueprint. The systematic steps are laid out in sequence and readers are walked through the process as though most interventions happened like that. In reality, they don't. But without an overall framework to work from, the consultant is tempted to play it by ear and risk floundering. As Lewis Carroll wrote in *Alice in Wonderland,* "If you don't know where you are going, any road will do." Readers are encouraged to understand the purpose of each step in the plan and its contribution to the success of the intervention, and then to use their own judgement about the procedures that will work best in their situation.

Any intervention or development project involves what can be called the words and the music. The words are *what* the project is trying to accomplish, its vision for the future. The music is *how* the project goes about accomplishing performance. But as the old saying goes, "They may know the words but they don't know the music." This book is about the music—happy humming!

Hedley G. Dimock
Puslinch, Ontario
November, 1992

The Intervention
and Collaborative
Change Model

The following pages describe the theory, strategies, and practices of collaborative interventions. During the sixteen years since the first edition was written, the pace of change has increased; so too has the interest in the specific kind of change that is based on collaboration. Although most of the changes in our communities and workplaces still arrive in an already determined form, an increasing percentage of them involve the people affected by the change in the process of making the change–the distinct component of collaborative change. It has proven to be the most effective way of rebuilding Eastern Europe, reframing the constitution in Canada, and managing the impact of the up-and-down economy on all organizations that serve our community.

The Intervention and Collaborative Change (ICC) model has the following three unique features:

1. It is based on an *intervention*;

2. The focus of change is on the *culture* of the community, work group, or organization; and

3. The members of the community, work group, or organization targeted for change participate and collaborate in all aspects of the change process.

An *intervention* is an "interference into a system or organization." In the Intervention and Collaborative Change model, this interference is planned and deliberate. Interventions have specific goals based on systematic planning and have selected strategies to maximize their impact and effectiveness. An intervention is an interruption into a system (community, work group, or organization) that produces some kind of a reaction. The impact of an intervention can range from very little to a great deal.

Think of the system targeted for change as a large body of water and the intervention as an intrusion breaking the placid surface (see Figure 1). Will the intervention create a ripple or a tidal wave?

Newton's Third Law of Motion states that to every action there is an equal and opposite reaction. This is a helpful way of looking at interventions; after looking at the input or interference of the intervention, you can look at the output or reaction to the interference. My experience demonstrates that Newton's Third Law is true but some reactions are delayed. An intervention may

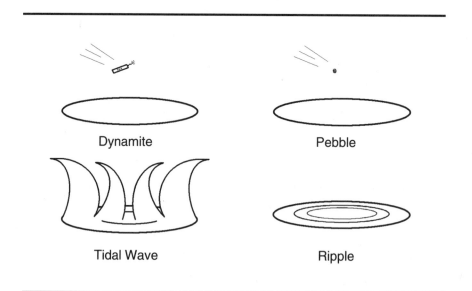

Dynamite

Pebble

Tidal Wave

Ripple

Figure 1. Interventions Can Cause a Ripple or a Tidal Wave

surprise and temporarily immobilize a system, or it may challenge the status quo in a way that takes time to think through. In planning and talking about interventions it may be helpful to describe them as ranging from "powder-puff" interventions to "dynamite" interventions (see Figure 2).

The second unique feature of the ICC model is that the focus of change is on the *culture* of the community, work group, or organization. A community, work group, or organization is a social system that over time develops communication patterns, group standards, and practices that are expected of all members. These usual ways of doing things are called the system's *culture*. The community, work group, or organization also has a history of successes and failures, including its skeletons in the closet or the things that are not talked about publicly. These can often predetermine the impact of an intervention—knowledge that came to me the hard way. Early in my career I was hired to lead a weekend retreat for the staff of a local high school at the beginning of the school year. We reviewed school goals and set up plans for the coming year and action groups to implement them. Great! But later that night I was told confidentially that the school did this every year as an exercise and that it was completely forgotten once they got back to school. The *culture* was one of posturing con-

---

Dynamite	Firecracker	Powder Puff
• A strategic plan refocusing the service delivery of the organization	• One-day team building with senior executives	• Parent-teacher study on new directions in education
• A community-supported plan for land use and waste disposal	• Outreach project targeting a new group of clients	• Community workshop on communication skills
		• Auditor's annual report

Figure 2. Sample Interventions

cerned teachers with no intention of changing the status quo. Clearly, the culture of the school would need to be changed before a revitalization and team-building workshop could have any impact.

A work group, community, or organization is a social system and this system is more than the sum of its parts. It has a culture or usual ways of doing things that determine a great deal of what its members will do. Trying to change individual members without changing the culture or norms of the social system to which they belong is not likely to be effective. Years ago many programs for treating juvenile delinquents withdrew them from their social systems and provided rehabilitation and retraining. The youth returned to their former social systems (community and gang) many months later with new skills and values and with a solid self-concept, yet most quickly reverted to their former ways. It was more important to be accepted by their peer groups than to continue using their newly learned skills and behaviors. Community-based delinquency prevention programs that focus on the social system as a whole and work at changing its culture are congruent with the ICC model.

Checking to see if a change program focuses on changing just individuals or the whole social system is a contrast that sharpens the culture-change principle. A child psychologist might work with a disturbed, acting-out adolescent as an individual to build confidence and increase self-awareness. Or the psychologist could work with the family as a whole, believing that the adolescent's behavior is influenced by family culture and is unlikely to change unless family norms and patterns change too.

It is likely that one of the reasons for the high success rate of Alcoholics Anonymous over medical-model treatment programs that focus on individuals is its creation of a new, primary social system with a non-drinking culture.

Clearly a social system is more than the sum of its parts. What changes in the service delivery or operation of Bell Canada occur when a new CEO takes over? Or what changes take place in a university or community college when the entire student body completely turns over every two or three years? There are few organizations I have worked with where I haven't heard, "If we could only get rid of old Harry (or old Hanna), we could really make some progress." Well, I've been around long enough now to see the old Harrys and Hannas come and go and to note no observable or recordable change in the system.

The education and development of individuals is not incompatible with a systems-change orientation. It is not an either-or situation. Individuals with sound problem-solving skills, social competencies, job-related abilities, and high self-esteem are likely to be happier and more productive whatever the culture. Yet for real changes to take place in the way things happen, more than the self-development of individuals needs to take place. The whole social-system culture within which they operate needs to change.

My own experiences, based on learning this principle, spurred my interest in a systems-change orientation and led five years later to the first edition of this book. In my early years I was very active in Human Relations Training. Because experiential learning dominated training in the late 1960s, I became concerned with the small effect it had on the way participating organizations were run. Northern Telecom, Alcan, the YMCA, and many other organizations exposed over three-quarters of their executives to this powerful training experience, yet little changed in the way things happened on the job. Human Relations Training's greatest impact was on helping participants to put their lives into perspective and to make personal-growth changes. They quit confining, bureaucratic jobs and left loveless, unfulfilling marriages. Those participants who worked in education adopted the exciting experiential learning method in their classrooms, but their schools and colleges maintained the same restrictive cultures.

The third unique feature of the ICC model is that the members of the community, work group, or organization plan, guide, implement, and evaluate the whole change process. The people who are affected by the change get to decide what happens to whom. This is a sharp contrast to many community-development and organizational-change programs in which whole new schemes of working are prepared and implemented by outsiders. New ideas and proposals for change are easy to create. Ask anyone who has been around for a while for suggestions for improvement and you will hear plenty. The trick is to get suggestions implemented and a change in the status quo to take place. The ICC model accomplishes this by giving ownership of the change program to the people in the targeted system. Involving the members in the planning and managing of the change not only gives them ownership but also increases the likelihood that they will carry out the program and gain support from one another in the process.

It is an adage among police officers that the laws can enforce only what the culture supports. Thus culturally unsupported laws (such as the speed limit on highways) are not obeyed because people don't believe in them or own them. The same concept is now influencing the way we change the culture that influences waste management, environment use, hunting, and fishing. It is considerably more successful and cost effective to involve the people affected by these programs in setting them up than to hire enforcers of a program decided by outsiders. One only has to look at the drug trade to see this concept in operation; a gigantic increase in enforcement and cost has not led to any decrease in use. On the positive side, drinking and driving practices have changed when the programs were owned by local anti-drinking and driving groups and norms changed.

Before moving on, it should be emphasized that this principle of involvement and ownership sounds good. It sounds democratic and humanitarian. Most people would support it on an opinion questionnaire but very, very few would organize a change program in which the participants decide who does what to whom. Even though many years of experience show that the ownership approach is the most cost effective as well as the most likely to succeed, few change agents have the personalities, values, and competencies to let other people own their interventions and change programs. With this in mind, the following pages will focus as much on the attitudes, beliefs, and well-being of the intervener as on the strategies, techniques, and skills of successful interventions.

Inasmuch as the ICC model uses collaboration as a major vehicle for change, the focus here will be mostly on interveners who do not have power over the change-program participants. These interveners may come from inside or outside the participating system. They may be called community developers, animateurs (animators), consultants, change agents, strategic planners, project coordinators, steering committee chairpeople, extension agents, or program facilitators. As people internal to the change system, they may come from the staff-development or personnel department in an organization, or in a community be president of a club or association. The thing they have in common is no position or organizational power to reward or punish the participants. People with position or organizational power are essentially managers or administrators, not consultants. Sometimes these managers go out posturing as consultants but they don't fool anyone for long–except maybe themselves. A common example is the government consultant who has grants to distribute or is a cog in the funding-distribution process. Few clients would give this person the time of day if he or she didn't have grants and funding to reward "good" behavior. Although managers will, of course, find the methods and techniques described here effective, the major focus is on the intervener-consultant who has to earn influence or power by being a helpful, trustworthy individual.

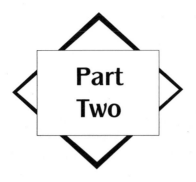

Part Two

Personal Qualities of the Intervener-Consultant

Years ago most interveners had technical skills that they brought to their change programs. Community developers in rural areas or Third World countries were agricultural specialists, drainage and irrigation specialists, engineers, doctors and nurses, or teachers. And consultants in organizations had technical skills in personnel planning, quality control, staff training, or records and communication. Often these consultants became surrogate managers or administrators because the people in power simply gave them a piece of the action and made them responsible for it.

During the past twenty years this picture has changed. The most effective consultants, who worked only from the influence they were able to earn as individuals, often had no professional training related to the content of their interventions. Sol Alinsky, one of the most famous community developers in North America, was reluctant to accept professionally trained community developers from schools of social work into his program because they had too much to unlearn to be able to relate to the people. Lately, the swing has been to hire people who are able to use their personal qualities as the major tools in facilitating change. The following list of personal qualities includes those that are most likely to give a consultant power and influence to get the job done well:

1. An ability to tune into your own feelings of how you are "here and now" and to share these feelings with others. If you are alienated from your own feelings, you are likely to be alienated from the feelings of others and restricted in your ability to give and to receive support.

2. The quality of getting in touch with the feelings of others and then being able to communicate back an accurate understanding of them.

3. A readiness to take risks–to tell others how you are feeling, to face negative feedback or hostility, to take a personal position on a controversial issue, and to risk losing a job. Perhaps the greatest risk is to listen to the ideas of others in such an open, understanding way that you may have to change your own beliefs.

4. A capacity to handle considerable uncertainty or even confusion and then shift comfortably to handle the very structured ways of the system.

5. An ability to manage authority and control. This means taking direction from others at some points, working collaboratively at other points, and yet being able to give leadership and direction when this would best serve the intervention's goals. Most interventions have a team of collaborators or a steering committee, and the intervener needs to give leadership to this group if it is to succeed.

6. A quality of open-mindedness and flexibility that enables the intervener to move through a variety of situations with all kinds of people and not get locked into right or wrong ways of doing things. This quality facilitates learning from the behavior and values of others. And it avoids the limiting approach of the dogmatic, judg-

mental person who always knows what is best for others and how they should solve their problems.

7. A talent for immediate response to situations and relationships. This means accepting new situations as they are found and moving quickly to establish and build relationships before looking at possible interventions. In these days of high mobility, temporary relationships, and attention spans epitomized by thirty-second television commercials, immediacy is the key. The intervener who is looking for more time to get to know people or moving a group to a more appropriate room for their meeting is likely to have been tuned out while the people go on to the next attraction. You need to build immediate personal support systems in your new situations to pull you through the difficult and often thankless tasks ahead.

8. Specific competencies or technical skills. Athletics, nursing, food preparation, craft work, and teaching are common examples. Excelling in such pursuits gives self-confidence and a winning outlook that successful consultants carry into their consulting roles.

Many training programs for consultants spend as much time on these personal qualities as on the strategies and techniques of intervention. This includes some of the university-based programs that include an exclusively personal-growth experience in their program. This is usually in the form of an experiential human relations program, a T-group laboratory, or a sensitivity-training group.

After you have looked over some of the personal qualities or skills of the consultant, you may want to add to or delete from the eight described. The specific number of qualities or which ones are included is not as important as the experience early in your reading of thinking about yourself and your likely strengths and weaknesses as a consultant. Hopefully too, at this point you will be clarifying your own learning goals as a consultant and what you would like to get out of this book.

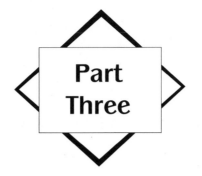

Part Three

Getting Ready for an Intervention

The following three questions should be answered before starting a program of change or development:

1. *What is your reason for the intervention?*
   Is there a specific change you would like to see implemented? Is it a content change (the program or the product) or a process change (the way people work)? Or are you interested in empowering a group of people and helping them to take on more responsibility for their community or job? Is it your job to organize new programs and you need some successes or are you a freelance consultant looking for some work? The clearer you are with yourself about the reason for your intervention, the more congruent you will appear in interpreting the rationale to others. Remember the earlier observation that posturing consultants do not fool people for very long.

2. *How much control do you want to have?*
   Do you want to control the major goals, the intervention process, or both? How much input and involvement, if any, do you really want to have from others? How ready

are you to accept a decision from the stakeholders to work on something you don't think would be useful? Look over Figure 3 as you go about answering these questions. Be ready to interpret your role to the system and the amount of control you expect to have. Dealing with control–who gets to do what to whom–is the most important and pervasive issue in any kind of a change or development program.

3. *What method of intervention will you use?*
Do you have a specific strategy in mind as you start the intervention? What kind of a role does the strategy set up for you? How consistent is it with the amount of control you want and your reason for the intervention? Most consultants have a strategy in mind as they start an intervention yet may be reluctant to surface it. They may be fearful that their plan will get vetoed, or they may think the "politically correct" position is to appear open-minded and eager for input from the stakeholders. Sharing thoughts and feelings, although risky, continues to be the behavior most likely to develop integrity and trust–the factors most likely to increase the consultant's personal influence in the intervention.

The most difficult of the three questions to answer before starting an intervention is the one about control. It is the most important and pervasive issue in an intervention and the hardest one to be up-front about. In my experience the control issue is where there is the greatest discrepancy between what interveners profess to believe and what they actually do.

In the community-development field and in many human-service organizations, there is a strong stigma attached to anything that sounds authoritarian or directive. Popular buzz words are "participative" and "collaborative"–words that sound democratic and humanistic. These expectations lead many interveners into posturing a low-control style in starting their interventions, a style

Amount of Control Associated with Different Styles of Interventions

DIRECTOR	EXPERT	CONSULTANT	RESOURCE	FACILITATOR	COLLABORATOR
• Makes decisions	• Diagnoses problem and tells what to do	• Provides data	• Helps group collect and analyze own data	• Helps with group process	• Joins system as a member or is one already
• Gives direction	• Has access to related systems	• Makes suggestions	• Trains group in planning skills	• Works as a catalyst	• Gives suggestions and enthusiasm
• Organizes others	• Uses superior knowledge and experience to control	• Shows alternatives	• Provides how-to-do-it resources	• May try to be neutral on issues	• Some influence that comes from value of contributions and prestige in group
• Has power to reward and punish		• Uses knowledge and experience in consultation with system		• Special status in group	
• Uses position to control the intervention		• Influence comes from respect and trust			
Examples: manager, executive, administrator	*Examples:* doctor, lawyer, computer expert	*Examples:* community developer, organization consultant	*Examples:* resource provider, group trainer	*Examples:* group observer and helper, process consultant	*Examples:* staff, board or community member interested in change

Figure 3. Control in an Intervention

that is not consistent with their real goals and predetermined strategies. In intervention slang it is a "We'll sucker them in and then slip it to them" strategy.

As I think of the hundreds of interveners for whom I have conducted training programs, I am always amazed at the answers that emerge when discussing the amount of control they want. "I'll just play it by ear when I get started with the people." "I'll leave it pretty well up to the group to define my role." "It will be a cooperative project with the people fully involved." I can't remember anyone ever saying, "Well, I'd really like to run the whole project as I think I know what would really be helpful."

At this point, I'd like to do my best to legitimize control interests. On the chart in Figure 3, I like to be a consultant with about half of the influence and control. As I often say to a steering committee of a development project, "We'll make all the decisions together but I expect to get two votes." Although I am often asked to take a facilitator role (with about 20 percent influence on the chart in Figure 3), I work like crazy to increase my relationships with the people and to make the most exciting process observations I can make to increase my influence. If I am getting heard only a bit more than anyone else in the system, why am I spending someone's money and my time here? Perhaps I could be much more influential and helpful working on another project—at least I wouldn't feel guilty about taking money and feeling I was doing so little in return.

Having said that, I'd also like to say that being a facilitator can be much more important than it seems. I discovered this while leading group guidance programs in a children's hospital. I would get a ward of twenty children involved in group activities that they would handle themselves; as I then had nothing to do, I would go and do some networking with the nurses or other staff. But if I were out of sight for more than a minute or two, the children's activities would cease. My presence provided the structure and security needed to empower the group to undertake some satisfying activity. In more recent years many steering committees would not meet if I weren't there, even though I would rarely say or do anything in the meeting. As my trainees often say, they feel very confident going ahead with all their interventions knowing that if there is a crisis I am around to come and help. And in thirty years of consulting there have probably been about six such crises–being a "do-little" enabler and backup can be an important role.

Most interventions start with a fair bit of control, which might come in the form of a directive from a board–"Let's develop a three-year strategic plan," or "It's time to implement a systematic performance appraisal program," or "We need to evaluate the effectiveness of our present service delivery." Or it might come in the form of an established way of working that the consultant brings. Community developers bring survey and interview methods along with public meetings; team builders bring preplanning activities, off-site meetings, and follow-up activities; and trainers bring needs analysis and a bag of usual programs or structured activities to meet the needs.

Kurt Lewin, the founder of group dynamics, once said that you could not introduce democracy by other than autocratic methods. In our Puslinch area of southern Ontario, Canada, we have two of the most successful auto factories in Canada–Honda and Toyota. The generally accepted reason for their success is their use of quality work circles, which is a team-building and worker-participation program. This program did not come into being because the workers (assisted by a consultant) came to management and said, "We want to be more involved in the decisions that affect us." Instead the program was a head-office directive. As the Honda and Toyota plants were set up, decisions about workspace layout and personnel hiring were based on the directive that there would be quality circles. Anyone who didn't want to go to meetings to plan work activities simply was not hired. A high level of control implemented this participative, collaborative program.

Another way to expand our thinking as we get ready to start an intervention is to review three contrasting intervention strategies. These are presented in Figure 4 and focus on directing, persuading, and problem solving. Actual, specific plans about starting the intervention should wait for the *Intervention Planning Guide* and a thorough consideration of the *Assumptions about Changing Social Systems*.

The choice of an intervention strategy is based on several considerations. First is the question of who is initiating the intervention. Is the intervener going to the system and making a proposal, or has the system asked for help with a specific problem? Another consideration is the importance of a specific, successful change to the intervener. The greater its importance, the more likely interveners will move to directing. Interveners will justify the directing strategy by saying things like "It is too important to leave to chance," or "The people are too inexperienced to handle this," or "There are too many people involved (or they are too busy) to make much participation feasible."

Yet another consideration is the amount of expertise the consultant thinks he or she has about the content of the change program. Often the more the consultant feels like an expert, the more he or she will want to structure the intervention and its likely impact. I am aware that this is often true for me as I find it easier to relax and problem solve with computer programmers and electronic engineers than with educators. I know little about computers and engineering; but with educators, I often am sure that I have more knowledge and job experience than anyone else in the room.

Another consideration in strategy selection is the status of the intervener in the system. For those with position, power, or very high status, the directive strategy is a feasible choice. Having easy entry into the system, such as being invited in, makes a persuading strategy attractive. If the system's problem is acute and people are ready to take action, the problem-solving strategy can generate unproductive frustration. On the other hand, interveners who are asking the system to let them come and help them and who have no status in the system may adopt the problem-solving strategy,

Style	Directing	Persuading	Problem Solving
Strategy	There is a preferred set of changes to be implemented or procedures to be followed.	Proposals for change are attractively presented to the group, and negotiations begin to gain their acceptance.	Procedures are proposed to look at how things are going, and discussions of any changes desired include all stake-holders.
Role of Intervener	The intervener lays out the changes to the group and works at developing or maintaining the power to carry them out.	Intervener works at selling the changes, demonstrating their effectiveness, lobbying for support, and making trade-off deals.	Intervener helps examine present practices, provides procedural resources, and monitors mutual decisions.
Assumptions	People need a clear plan and strong leadership. Experts are qualified to make changes.	People should have a say in change. People will change if they know why they are doing things.	Those people affected by a change are best able to make it. Change is best brought about through collaborative, consensual agreements.
Skills	Concrete organizing, evaluating, rewarding, and punishing.	Sales ability, persuasion, and negotiation.	System scanning, problem solving, group building, communicating, and planning.
Strengths	Changes are what intervener wants. Little time lag in starting on changes. Everyone knows what is expected.	Complete proposals can be presented to group. Feedback from group may improve plans. Involvement reduces resistance to change.	Almost assured of change in some respect. System learns procedures to make further changes. Increased responsibility and satisfaction within group.
Weaknesses	Independent judgment and creativity stifled. Implementation may be sabotaged or avoided. Antagonism may spill over elsewhere.	Implementation may be spotty as it depends on acceptance of changed plans and development of new skills and attitudes.	Change may be inappropriate or ineffective. Process may be time consuming. People may become more important than the task.

Figure 4. Intervention Strategies

which is safer and doesn't risk having any of their proposals rejected. Other interveners with several personal contacts in the system, a reputation in the field that gives them status, or a sponsoring organization that establishes their credibility are likely to have a wider range of choices.

The personal qualities of the intervener also influence the selection of an intervention strategy. Consultants who have difficulty handling frustration and ambiguity lean toward strategies that are high on structure, in which goals and action time lines can be part of a flow chart. Consultants who rate low in their readiness to take direction and control from others won't be attracted to helping senior managers implement their pet programs. And those who fear rejection and avoid taking sides may prefer the neutral and conflict-avoiding strategy of problem solving. The perfect choice lies less in the specific strategy and more in the intervener's readiness to be up-front about it and show congruent behavior.

Assumptions About Changing Social Systems

Over the years a number of assumptions about changing social systems have evolved from research in the field and from practical experience. These assumptions have been very helpful in planning interventions, guiding implementation practices, and giving insight into components of successful and unsuccessful projects.

1. *The social system (community, work group, or organization) is the focus of change.*

When people meet in groups or communicate regularly, they develop usual ways of doing things. These procedures of operation develop into group norms and group values. The clearer people are about these norms, the more they know what is expected of them, what they can expect from others, and what they need to do to get ahead. This makes it easier for members of a system to work together toward the same goal. Clarity of norms and values and the consistency with which they operate contribute to community or organization excellence.

For example, a hockey team on which everyone knows the procedures of operation will consistently win over an all-star team of equally good players who have less teamwork. Excellence is the result of every player's knowing what is expected on the ice personally and for every other player and knowing the punishments and rewards forthcoming if the expectations are or are not achieved.

It is very difficult to change the behavior of individuals operating in a social system without changing the norms or standards of the group, especially if such change would make people deviate from the norms. As the norms are the property of the group as a whole, they cannot easily be changed except by the group as a whole. An individual or subgroup, even with a great deal of power, usually cannot change them. Thus, the most successful approach is to change the norms of the system so it will support the new behaviors of system members. This explains what typically happens to the innovative teacher who is given encouragement to work on a new program. As soon as the new program upsets the usual way of working or values, the teacher experiences pressure from the rest of the school staff to conform and ends up either leaving the school or dropping the new program. Experimental programs are doomed to failure unless they can modify the norms of the larger system.

2. *Those people affected by a change should be involved in making that change.*

This assumption is often considered as a philosophical point of view in keeping with democratic ideals and nonmanipulative ethics. Now it is presented as a pragmatic assumption based on considerable experience and research. When I received my doctorate from Columbia University and was ready to change the world, I could not understand why organizations were not interested in making improvements based on recent research and other facts. It took a long time to learn that people and social systems do not have much interest in the ideas or proposals of others; rather, they are busy working on their own interests. This is why practice always lags years behind knowledge; the case of the fluoridation of water to prevent tooth decay is a good example. This procedure was recommended by the Canadian dental and medical associations forty years ago, yet the practice has been implemented slowly. Soon I found that good ideas were really common. Any group could produce a long list of possible improvements. The real trick was to get some implementation of any of the proposals. The best way to do this was to involve the people in analyzing how things were going, setting targets for change, and working out implementation procedures.

Even when a decision has been made or a goal set, those affected can still be involved in working out the implementation. For example, managers might be told, "Your two departments are going to be amalgamated. Would you start planning how this can best be done and on what kind of a timetable?" It is quite clear to me that I have the choice as an intervener of working on high-quality change plans (ones I have initiated), knowing that there is little likelihood that they will be implemented, or working on possibly lower quality plans (theirs) knowing there is a good chance that they will be implemented (see Figure 5).

Change of social systems will be facilitated to the degree the intervener helps those affected by the change to become involved in discussing the change, developing anawareness of the need for change, and feeling some ownership over the implementation procedures. Self-diagnosis and goal setting with the group encourage this involvement and will ensure that the pressure for change will be within the group.

There are no perfect strategies; each has its strengths and weaknesses. Successful interveners select whatever seems most appropriate to the situation and comfortable to them. The success lies in the intervener's ability to be up-front about the choice.

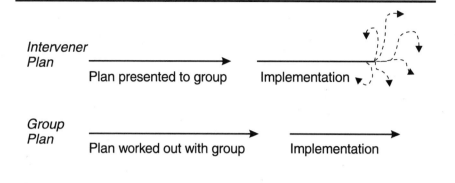

Figure 5. External Versus Internal Planning for Change

3. *Possibilities for change are increased if the group is functioning well.*

Well-functioning groups have high levels of trust and acceptance among members, open communication, and personal satisfaction in being members. Such groups also have the cohesion to make decisions and expect that members will take responsibility for implementing them. If the social system that is the target for change is a loose-knit collection of people, effort will be in order to help them to become a group and to be able to take ownership and responsibility for improving the system. The group can then develop clearer standards and norms that can be used to sustain any changes that are made by the group. Weak groups put the intervener in the role of facilitating group building during an early or middle phase of the intervention.

The more attractive a group is to a person, the greater his or her acceptance of the group norms and readiness to work on changes planned by the group. People who trust one another are also more likely to explore openly everyone's opinions of the change plans. This will make use of all the resources in the group and encourage the expression of negative feelings, which in turn will clarify the commitment to change and reduce resistance.

Effective communication among members will also improve interpersonal relations and increase member satisfaction with the group. This in turn will make the group more cohesive and thus more able to influence behavior.

4. *The power people in the system must support the change or it has little chance of success.*

Although change may not need to start at the top, it is essential that the person or people in power support the change. Even though the power person may not be able to bring about change unilaterally, power can prevent or sabotage changing group norms. This is especially true when the power person has an administrative capacity and can control certain areas such as budget allocation in the system. For twenty-five years, I have said that I wouldn't work on a change program unless the head person of the system was actively involved. Although I have deviated from this principle quite a few times, only twice was I not sorry. In these two cases the systems-change intervention focused on the middle-status people and worked with them for a long enough time that when they advanced to the top positions they were able to implement the changes we had worked on.

5. *Change in one part of a system will produce strain in related parts and require changes in them.*

A social system is more than the sum of its parts; it is a gestalt where the parts have special meaning because of the whole. Thus, changing one part creates a dissonance within the whole and if the whole doesn't change, the part will be pressured to return to the status quo.

Bavelas (1961) reports on a change program that failed because it succeeded too well. Workers in one part of a production line found ways to improve their performance. Their production increased considerably and as they were paid by the piece, so did their wages. The increased production at one point in the assembly line produced a pile-up in front of it and a vacuum of parts behind it. In addition the workers were making much more money than their colleagues. Neither could be tolerated by the system and the successful changes were discontinued.

An early case study of change in the YMCA demonstrated the effects of trying to change one part of the system. Sorenson and Dimock (1955) expressed their findings as follows: "No part of institutional change is an island unto itself: changes in program call for changes in every other part of the institution... and advance in one sector cannot proceed far ahead of change in other sectors... changes in staff goals and ways of working are dependent upon administrative procedures, policies, and budgets, which in turn require changes in Boards and Committees."

The interventions I've been part of have had the same experiences with systems change, so much so that we carefully monitor the changes in the staff roster during and after our intervention as an indicator of impact. No matter what the focus of the intervention, there is a good chance it will affect promotions and severances if real changes are going forward. In fact, one of the ways in which we are surest that something is happening in one of our interventions is through the repercussions from other parts of the system. If we have put on a demonstration program in a school with four or five of the teachers and at the end of a year none of the other teachers knows about the project or has any feelings about it, we can be sure we've had little influence on the school system. Paraphrasing Newton's Third Law of Motion, we could state that "for every social intervention action there should be an equal reaction from other parts of the system."

6. *Previous interventions in the social system establish a pattern of response to further interventions.*

Sarason (1967) documented this insight a number of years ago, which made sense out of several experiences I had had that left me puzzled. A typical example was the high school that each fall held a staff meeting. It was just an exercise; no one took it seriously and nothing happened as a result of it. It was a pleasant day for the staff and provided some professional-development window dressing. One year they asked me to come to help them with the day. Although a planning committee worked up the program based on a needs assessment, and we retired to a country resort for two days to work, I could not understand the lack of follow-through on the work that was done. Sarason's theory (a theory being a summary of many experiences) helped me to explore a likely possibility of the previous pattern continuing to unfold.

Interveners would do well to take a little time and do some data collection on previous intervention experiences with particular focus on who did what to whom and how it worked out. Then if they learn of a series of disastrous experiences with community developers or management consultants, they will have another slant on the hostility they encounter on first entering the system. Or, if a series of previous interventions have all fizzled and died, they can suspect that a self-fulfilling prophecy is at work that may influence their intervention.

7. *Resistance to change is normal and helpful in stabilizing new changes.*

It is my experience that workers' reactions to a proposed change can be divided into the following three categories:

ENTHUSIASTS: They appear to be the avant-garde who are very progressive and see change in itself as a good thing. Although I find it pleasant to receive such immediate positive support, I find these people don't usually stick with what we are doing; rather they run on to something else that is new and different. Their enthusiasm is an image and lacks guts.

REJECTERS: These people don't consider new possibilities. They're locked into an established pattern, often out of fear, and refuse to examine it. They are closed to change and will not even try out something different on an experimental basis.

RESISTERS: They look at any new ways of doing things very skeptically and want to be shown how well it works. They will try something experimentally and drop it if it is not an improvement on what they were doing. They move slowly, checking everything out along the way. But once they move, resisters are as committed to that new action as they were to their previous practices. Thus, they will examine very carefully any later attempts to change the product of our intervention and in this way help to stabilize the progress made.

At a personal level, resistance to change is healthy as it gives some equilibrium and stability to our lives. Too little resistance leaves a person "blowing with the wind" and too much creates a rigidity that blocks off any adjustment to changing conditions, which is equally unhealthy. Gestalt psychology suggests that the social system also responds with resistance to change over and above that encountered on a personal level. Resistance to change also helps to perpetuate the social system and to keep it healthy. Although resistance appears to slow down the movement in the early stages of an intervention and although it can be frustrating, it gives guts and stability to movement in later stages of the intervention. It is to the intervener's advantage to encourage the expression of this resistance and then use it to test feasibility and evaluate the usefulness of the change.

8. *Change is more easily effected by reducing the forces against change than by strengthening the forces for it.*

Situations involving change can be analyzed by looking at the forces for and against change that tend to balance out and keep activity at a given level. Consider the university professor in a publish or perish atmosphere. Publishing more may mean a promotion, recognition, and the satisfaction of owning part of a book or journal. Yet a number of factors balance these forces, such as the solitary nature and loneliness of writing, the knowledge that relatively few people ever read professional journals, the ease with which writing can be postponed, and the possibility of not being published. Considering the balance of these factors, the professor will probably write about one article every year or two.

This force-field analysis can be pictured as a giant tug-of-war, with the supporting forces pulling on one side and all the restraining forces on the other. In a force field related to my smoking behavior, the restraining forces easily overpower the supporting forces and I don't smoke, although a couple of times sustaining forces increased and I actually considered it. An associate smokes between one and two packs a day, depending on the balance of his forces at that moment. If tension increases, other smokers arrive, and so on, his smoking increases; if we are alone and he is busy driving the car or washing dishes, the smoking decreases. Thus the balance is not static or routine habit, but dynamic, changing with the balance of forces.

I have saved this assumption about change until last, for of all the concepts from the social sciences, I have used this one most frequently and with the most success. Most of my consulting work has had a group doing a force-field analysis and then planning specific strategies to reduce the factors restraining the proposed change. In my early days as a student counselor and now in my executive coaching, the force field is used to assess the pros and cons of any action being considered. Exploring "what is the worst thing that could happen" clarifies the fears and blockages and frees the way to constructive planning.

Considering our tug-of-war analogy, increasing the supporting forces would be like adding more members or stronger ones to that side of the rope. The other team will now have to resist harder, dig their heels in or lie down in their effort to hang on. However, if one side stopped pulling and let go of the rope, the other side could no longer resist–there would be nothing to pull against. Rather than arguing about the pros and cons of a particular action, the merits of both sides are discussed and to further test the feasibility of the proposed action both strategize how, if at all, they could reduce the restraining forces. If they are successful in figuring out how to remove or reduce the blockages, the proposal will be free to move forward.

This suggests that in getting ready for an intervention the intervener will profit from doing an analysis of the change program using a force-field approach and then considering ways of reducing the factors against the change. Figure 6 depicts one possible force-field analysis of whether or not you finish reading this book. Depending on how the forces balance for you, you will stop reading, read a bit more, or read a lot more. The wavy line in the middle tries to highlight the idea that the balance of forces may be continually shifting. The balance at this moment is that you will continue reading, but in five minutes the notion of an ice-cold drink may get to you and you'll stop. In a complex social system, it is likely that the balance of forces has set a pattern that became institutionalized and will be much harder to change.

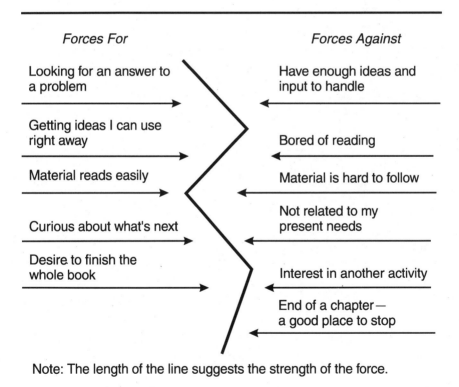

Forces For	Forces Against
Looking for an answer to a problem	Have enough ideas and input to handle
Getting ideas I can use right away	Bored of reading
Material reads easily	Material is hard to follow
Curious about what's next	Not related to my present needs
Desire to finish the whole book	Interest in another activity
	End of a chapter — a good place to stop

Note: The length of the line suggests the strength of the force.

Figure 6. Balance of Forces to Continue Reading

Starting an Intervention

Commitment to Planning

The starting place for an intervention is a commitment to a planning process. Planning, as part of preparing for an intervention, sharpens the goals, improves the choice of a particular action plan, and increases the likelihood of others collaborating in the intervention. Sometimes interveners resist planning by saying things like "Let's keep it spontaneous" or "We'll play it by ear." These are often attempts to maintain control over the intervention as our spontaneous impulses tend to be more self-centered and autocratic than our reflective thinking. And unplanned interventions imply that there are no conceptual frameworks or intervention skills that can be used to increase the effectiveness of the intervention.

Interveners may also resist early planning because they feel they are taking unfair advantage of the others who will be involved later by having a plan worked out ahead of time. This is a good point; yet I feel that having a plan clarifies what the intervener has in mind in a way that others can see it and react to it. If the intervener is prepared to modify or even scrap the original plan, that is the real test of openness to the input of others. In the posturing-of-spontaneity approach, the intervener has the same ideas and biases but they remain hidden from others and thus closed to any modification.

Is an Intervention the Best Approach?

The next concern in considering an intervention is determining if it is the most useful way to proceed at this point. Is an interference into the social system focusing on norms and usual ways of doing things likely to be more effective than a demonstration project or a staff-training program? The rule of thumb for deciding is determining whether the desired goal is chiefly determined by the norms of the system or by the behavior and skills of the workers. The former suggests a systems intervention and the latter some kind of educational program. Alternatively, a skill-training program or a values clarification exercise may be the best place to start. Such an activity would establish the credibility of the intervener, energize the system, and give the potential participants some of the tools that would be helpful in the intervention. Sometimes an appropriate place to start is a speech at a public meeting, an article or letter to the editor in the local newspaper, or a demonstration at a staff conference. Many of my interventions have started with an informal visit to the community or a tour of the organization just to see and be seen. Working this all out may take some time and exploration of the system. Dynamite interventions into the whole system are not necessarily the best way to go.

Studies are continually emerging that show new areas of individual behavior that are heavily influenced by social systems. My earlier booklets have reported how eating habits, childcare practices, production rates in factories, and individual perceptual judgments are affected by group norms. Agricultural representatives have moved away from the experimental-farm approach and now intervene in rural communities in an effort to modernize farming practices. Public-health nurses and community psychologists have found it more effective to intervene in the social system than to work just with individuals. Drug use, delinquency, and sexual behavior are also closely related to social systems. And the apparent failure of school integration in the United States through busing also says a lot about social systems and social change.

Testing the Social System

As an intervention idea germinates, it may help to explore the community or organization that is the focus of the intervention and test its readiness to get involved in or receive the intervention. Or, if a group or structure related to the intervention area does not exist, what would be needed to put one together? We may want to institute a new performance-appraisal system in the organization and will need to work out how we can get an action-oriented planning committee together. An awareness of the receptivity of the system to the proposed intervention will help to plan strategy and the appropriate role for the intervener(s).

In reviewing the social system some thought should be given to the best entry point. Starting at the top is the single best entry point, but it may be passed over if there is a very receptive group in the organization or if the top is likely to stop any further planning or action. Focusing on the point of greatest stress in the system is another possibility. Some interveners like to talk to a full cross section of people in the system before they see the power person, in order to have some clearly defined needs and problems to discuss. Another strategy is to enter at the weakest or most receptive point and build up a following or power group before moving on to the rest of the system. This strategy, using the domino theory, is usually chosen by people wanting to start a revolution.

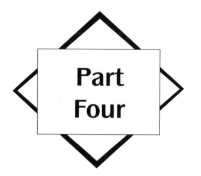

Part Four

Outline for an Intervention

Although one outline will not fit all situations, most interventions include five phases: (1) entry; (2) data collection; (3) data analysis and goal setting; (4) action taking and stabilizing change; and (5) evaluation and replanning (Figure 7).

Entry

1. A brief description of the situation and the objectives of the intervention.

2. An overview of the social system (a power analysis and force-field analysis are helpful here) and its expectations for the intervention.

3. Gaining entry into the system and establishing credibility for this intervention.

4. Negotiating about how the project will be started (who will have what roles and responsibilities, who will pay for what, time parameters, closure, evaluation, and follow-up procedures).

5. Group building (trust and commitment) with the steering committee.

	Which stakeholders can we involve in this activity?	Who should be informed of this activity?	How will this activity be done?	Timetable for this activity?	What special resources are needed for this activity?
INITIAL PLANNING (Focus and parameters of the intervention)					
ENTRY • Overview of target system • Negotiating project • Building credibility					
DATA COLLECTION • Needs • Power in system • Leverage points • Group functioning • Internal and external norms					
GOAL SETTING • Data analysis • Involvement • Setting priorities					
ACTION PLANNING • Gaining commitment • Reducing resistance • Impact on other parts of system					
ACTION TAKING • Stabilizing action • Closure or follow-up					
EVALUATION & REPLANNING (Maintaining a continuous process)					

Figure 7. Guide Sheet for Planning an Intervention

Data Collection

6. Deciding who should be involved in looking at the change possibilities. This step may benefit from collecting data on who has power and influence in the system and who would be affected by the changes likely to be forthcoming.

7. Finding out the interests and needs of these people and their previous experience with interventions and consultants. Locating the leverage points in the social system.

8. Assessing the present functioning of the group or organization with reference to communication, norms, status differences, sex roles, and power.

Data Analysis and Goal Setting

9. Finding ways to involve the appropriate people in analyzing the data, setting the goals, and establishing priorities. These goals will be most useful if they are specific, realizable, and immediate.

10. Additional training may be indicated at this phase (or at the entry phase) in group building and increasing the effectiveness of existing decision-making procedures.

Action Taking

11. Gaining acceptance and commitment for action from the system. Dealing with resistance to change and impact on other parts of the system.

12. Periodic review of progress and celebration of accomplishments.

13. Providing follow-through procedures. Stabilizing the new actions and the process of planned change.

Evaluation and Replanning

14. Assessing the impact and usefulness of the intervention (productivity and worker satisfaction) and building in a

continuous planning procedure based on this new data collection. Establishing closure.

Power Analysis

Understanding where the power is in a community or organization and how it is distributed provides perspective for determining the point of entry into the system and selecting a strategy for intervention. It may also help with deciding if an intervention is the way to work with this system and if this is an appropriate time to start.

The necessity of the power people in the system participating in the intervention is one of our eight assumptions about facilitating change. Power is the ability to influence what happens in the system. Its source may be the trust and respect an individual or subgroup has earned, a position that gives power to reward and punish, or access to money or funding. Prestige power is based on the track record an individual has of helping to accomplish tasks and solve problems and of supporting people. People with prestige power are natural leaders in the system and may be most useful in helping an intervention, especially if the person or people in position power lack acceptance and credibility.

The easiest way to identify the people with prestige power is to do a "reputation ranking" (Figure 8). A sample of people in the community or organization are asked to name the three or four people whose influence and support should be gained by any new project or program hoping to be successful. After every six people have reported their nominations the results are tabulated on a master list. Usually after five or six groups of people–thirty to thirty-six people in total–have given their nominations, the same names will occupy the top ranks of those nominated most frequently. When the further addition of names does not change the rank order of names at the top of the master list, the procedure is stopped with a very good assurance that the influence structure has been identified.

Reputation Nomination

If a new program were to be started here, who are the 3 or 4 people whose support would most likely ensure its success?

1. _____

2. _____

3. _____

4. _____

Figure 8. Reputation Nomination

Position power goes with whatever hierarchy exists in the community or organization and is best analyzed by looking at an organizational chart or organogram and then highlighting the key positions or people with special power. Figure 9 shows what this looked like in one of our interventions.

People can also have power through their control of computer systems, communication channels, and discretionary monies or funding sources. Examples are the personnel director who controls who is suggested for open positions, the editor of the community newsletter who decides what articles will be published, and the chairperson who decides what items will be on the agenda of the next meeting. Money, products, people, or services that people need to do their jobs or enhance their life styles are powerful sources of power. An amazing example of this occurred when I worked at a university with a third-rate library. A newly arrived head librarian convinced the faculty council that all new courses proposed had to have library approval before they could be considered for acceptance. The library, in theory, would determine if the course had adequate library holdings to support it. Naturally few did and departments had to give larger parts of their budgets to the library to acquire the books and journals. And if a

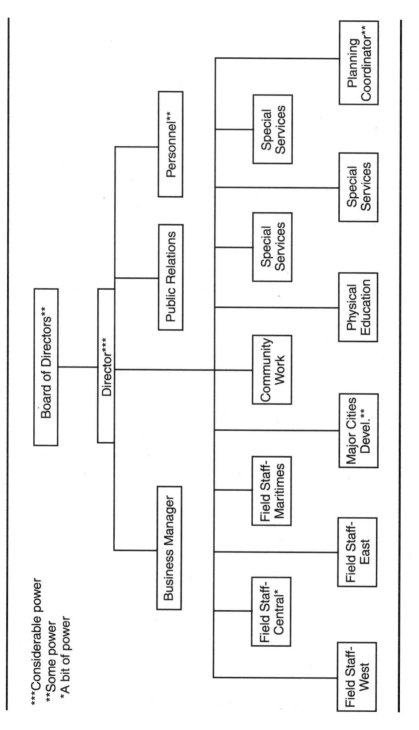

Figure 9. National Office of a Community-Serving Organization

***Considerable power
**Some power
*A bit of power

Board of Directors**

Director***

Business Manager

Public Relations

Personnel**

Field Staff-Central*

Field Staff-Maritimes

Community Work

Special Services

Special Services

Field Staff-West

Field Staff-East

Major Cities Devel.**

Physical Education

Special Services

Planning Coordinator**

department did not cooperate, the library delayed the report indefinitely. Inasmuch as the university was in a period of very rapid development, it moved the library from a position of little power to one of the key players in development for the two years the procedure lasted.

Some systems have two separate power structures, one formal or official and the other informal. A hospital I worked in had an official structure with a figurehead president and doctor as chief of staff; the real day-to-day power was with the director and nursing administration. With school boards, the school trustees have the official power. However, because the administration controls all meeting agendas and minutes, as well as everything the trustees get to see or read, administration runs the show. In addition to these systems in which there is a stated but not powerful structure on paper and a really powerful structure behind the throne, some communities have an underground, alternative power structure that people do not know much about and probably would not accept if they did. These may take the form of unelected chambers of commerce, religious groups, service clubs, pressure groups, voters' associations, criminal gangs, or the kind of counter-culture we saw in the 1960s. Tom Peters (1982), co-author of *In Search of Excellence,* says that in all the major companies he studied, the research-and-development departments never came up with a major product breakthrough. Rather, breakthroughs all came from underground "skunk works" whereby people surreptitiously used their time and "liberated" supplies and equipment for their secret projects.

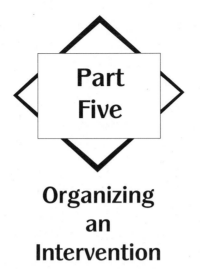

Part Five

Organizing an Intervention

Entry

Let us start looking at the entry process by describing three dimensions that usually determine our entry point and strategy. The first is "Who is initiating the intervention?" Being asked by the system to come and help is an entirely different entry than charging into a system with a dynamite intervention. A community that is in poor shape is not likely to find you and invite you in, for if they could manage that they would not be in such desperate shape. And if the community is of a different language group in a Third World country, it would be impossible. Really unhealthy organizations are also unlikely to mobilize themselves and their financial resources to come and hire you. Interveners prepared to wait for invitations from the system to resolve their entry are likely ruling out working with the most needy systems. This is also true for internal consultants–those programs, people, or departments most in need are the least likely to invite you in.

The second dimension is the possibility of a triangular entry. Person A hires you (Person B) to lead a development program for Group C. This is the situation when you join Canadian University Service Overseas or Katimavik (Canada's domestic peace corps), or do a project for the Canadian International Development Agency–they send you to help a group of people who may not know you are coming, much less want you. And I have frequently been hired by the chief executive officer (CEO) to go and turn around a department that the CEO thinks needs help. This can even get more complicated if the group that the CEO has hired you to help works for or is responsible to another system. As an example, the Canadian government might hire a consultant to introduce new farming practices to agricultural specialists in Sierra Leone, who are employed by the Canadian government.

The third dimension affecting entry point is the level in the system that entry is most feasible. Many powerful interventions are concocted in informal sessions between a person or subgroup in the system and the would-be intervener. The question is where in the system is that person or subgroup in terms of influence? For example, when you go to Hanna's office to pick her up for lunch, she is with her supervisor, Estelle. Estelle says, "Oh yes, you wrote that book on revitalizing work groups. Boy, could we use your help here!" Now you have a potential entry point in the system, but Estelle is two layers down from the CEO. The challenge now is to get in through Estelle but involve the CEO in the process (Assumption 4–the power in the system must support the change or it has little chance of success).

Recently I made an intervention that got started in much the same informal way. I was meeting with Barney, a graduate student, about his thesis. During our luncheon he mentioned that I should do one of the university's Friday colloquiums. I said I'd be delighted. Barney was the student representative on the department council and his thesis supervisor was in charge of the Friday guest lectures. When Barney asked what I might talk about, I suggested we have an experiential learning session on facilitating cultural change and use the department as a case study. Now the challenge was to plan an exciting intervention and stimulate interest in follow-up–as well as to make sure the key players in the department were in the room.

If the contact person in the system has access to the decision-making process, as Barney did, entry can be accomplished quickly and easily. If not, perhaps that person can involve someone in an informal discussion that can access the system. It is likely Hanna's supervisor Estelle could arrange such a discussion with her agency head.

While considering these three dimensions and deciding on entry strategy, keep in mind that during the entry phase you may have more leverage than later in the intervention. It is similar to being interviewed for a new job. It is easier to negotiate an extended vacation, or working a day a week at home during the give-and-take of the interview than after you are in harness and subject to the usual norms of the system. The negotiations of the entry phase also set the norms for the rest of the project. Collaborative planning, participant involvement, your authentic behavior, and processing the intervention are best started now if they are to be part of it later on. Let me stress this by saying that I am weak in the entry phase, especially with my high trust in working things out later and my enthusiasm to get into the action. Yet every intervention that I felt dissatisfied with later had failed during the entry phase.

For example, when someone hires me to work with someone else, I try to involve the other people in the decision about my working with them. But this is easier said than done. In my confident, high-risk mode, I have said to a CEO that I would work with him and his five senior executives only if I met with the total group, outlined my thoughts and feelings about the intervention, and all five agreed that they wanted me to come and work with them (one was undecided and asked for a second meeting before agreeing). With larger groups I've asked for a 75-percent mandate to do the project (I do not have the nerve to ask for 100 percent with a large group). But often I enter without involvement or proper contracting and regret it later.

For example, as a favor to a former student, I agreed to do a one-day team building with the agency for which she was staff-development coordinator. I did not check that everyone was on board (especially the CEO). I did not have any involvement or input from the staff, and I did not clarify expectations for the day. I outlined a suggested day that involved everyone. I was told that this day was an annual event and that the last two had been failures, which was why they really wanted me this year. However, I didn't look into the pattern set up by these failures (all that after twenty-five years of consulting). On the team-building day we waited over an hour for the CEO to arrive, and when he did, he proceeded to plan the day–as we all should have done two weeks before. The result was the staff got to air problems that were frustrating them. It was great catharsis; but without any plans to change anything, it was just a gripe session with everyone back in the same rut the next day. This was the posturing training event that participants had taught me twenty years before; I had missed it in skirting the entry negotiations and trying to save them money.

In working out the negotiating or contracting aspects of the entry phase, a "give/get" activity is a popular choice. Participants in the change program write down what they are prepared to give to the program and what they would like to get out of it. The consultant does this too, and all lists are shared with the total group. Some kind of a summary is prepared and it is used to clarify and document expectations and responsibilities for this intervention. It also makes a splendid evaluation tool as it can be brought out from time to time to see how things are going. Doing a "give/get" not only achieves a very helpful kind of participant involvement in the entry phase but it also encourages early collaboration in intervention planning such that the project is seen to be owned 50/50 by the consultant and the participants. Hopefully the participants or stakeholders will feel that they have the control they need over how the project will proceed.

Some kind of documentation of expectations and parameters of the intervention–time, money, resources, and tasks to be included–is helpful to clarify these areas and to reduce misunderstandings that may be due to forgetfulness. I avoid specific signed contracts as I hope to model trust and work on mutual interests, but I often write letters of intent that outline the parameters as I understand them from our negotiations. Knowing it is hard to estimate these parameters—especially the time needed—before the intervention starts, I usually build in a "change-of-scope" meeting. This meeting takes place about two-thirds of the way through the project and is a time to review how things are going and what parameters, if any, should be renegotiated.

Any activity has two elements—*what it is people are doing and how they are doing it*. They are usually referred to as the *content* and the *process*, or the *task* and the *relationships*. Consultants, especially those outside the system, have a corner on the process market. Up-front, authentic consultants are always sharing how they feel about the way things are going and are initiating processing activities. At the end of a negotiating meeting the consultant will say, "Let's take ten minutes and talk about how we worked and how we felt during this meeting." A more thorough half-hour should be spent at the conclusion of the entry phase with suggested questions to respond to or a short process-oriented questionnaire to be completed by the participants. One group of project participants formalized this in its culture as the "meeting after the meeting." At the end of the regular meeting planning for the intervention—content and task—the group would sit around informally and chat about how the meeting had gone and how they felt about their parts in it. Soon they were giving each other feedback about their roles and building a very solid intervention team.

As the entry phase moves toward completion, it is timely to establish the procedures that will move the intervention into its next phases. Every intervention must have some person or group who will champion the change program. The best person is the formal or informal power person as revealed by a power analysis based on the reputation-nomination technique. The most frequent choice, however, is a steering committee or project task force. Five to eight members is the most effective size; using the nominal group-size theory, they should be the people whose contributions will most likely get the job done. They are not representatives of constituents or subgroups in the system, but are carefully chosen for their knowledge, skill, and influence in the system. The power analysis described previously provides suggested norms for this committee. Our seventh assumption about changing systems suggests a balance of "enthusiasts" and "resisters" makes the best mix and that any "rejecters" should be eliminated even if they do appear to have influence.

When the target system is a large community, it is likely more useful to establish two groups–a large constituent assembly or representative council and a small steering committee that makes recommendations to the general assembly. Some community field workers prefer to use a general assembly to coordinate the process and small task forces to pick up the planning for the various objectives identified. The new steering committee or task force will need an orientation to the intervention process that models the way the consultant hopes to work with the group throughout the intervention. Starting with a lecturette and show-and-tell by the consultant is not the way to go to model the ICC requirement of extensive participant involvement and 50/50 ownership of the project. Team-building activities and probably some training in problem solving and decision making are also in order. A lot of the intervention's success is riding on the effective functioning of this group.

In summary, a desirable entry phase using the Intervention and Collaborative Change model has the following components:

- Clear descriptions of expectations and responsibilities (give/get);

- Extensive involvement of the participants;

- Participation of power person(s) or subgroups;

- Considerable modeling of concern for process with regular process evaluations; and

- Participants' feeling that they will have the control they need over the process.

The most usual error in the entry phase is to reduce it by trying to cut costs. This was the experience I illustrated in my example of the favor to the former student, who only had a budget to pay for my one-day team building. Although I gave in that time, I had learned years before to respond to this problem by helping clients find the money. If they were community-serving organizations, I'd put them in touch with the government or foundations that were interested in supporting their programs. And if they were business or industry organizations, I'd offer to postpone part of my payment until the next year's budget, believing that if they wouldn't put some money into next year's budget they had to admit it was a very low priority.

My initial learning on this was with an organization that had twenty-five people ready to go on a leadership-training program but they only had $3,000 available to pay for a two-and-one-half day program (which took about seven days of my time with planning meetings, preparation, and follow-up). I've never forgotten my astonishment at having two participants tell me on day two that they had to leave early to attend a leadership-training program (costing the agency at least $4,000 each). So much for tight budgets. Or as my colleague Bob Crook used to say, "Tell me how you spend your money, and I'll tell you what your priorities are."

Interveners need to put value on the contracting, negotiating, and participant-involvement components of the entry phase and charge for it in their allocation of time and budget monies for the project. Submitting a tender bid for a project not only puts no value on the negotiating part of entry but is not compatible with the involvement and joint ownership philosophy of the Intervention and Collaborative Change model.

Data Collection and Analysis

Three concerns about data collection include the following: (1) What data should we collect? (2) How should we collect and analyze them? and (3) Who should do it? If the community or organization has approached the consultant for help, there will analyze them? and (3) Who should do it? If the community or organization has approached the consultant for help, there will be a "presenting problem" expressed. This problem, which may or may not be the real problem, is the logical place to start in framing issues that should be investigated in the data-collection process. But if it is an intervener-initiated process, then the ICC model suggests that the target system will identify the data that should be collected. The consultant will assist in suggesting profitable areas to investigate or supply several usual tools for stimulation but the final selection of issues will come from the participants.

Figure 10 reviews methods of data collection and contrasts some of their strengths and weaknesses. The most frequently used methods of collecting data are individual interviews and survey questionnaires. However, group-interview methods are more compatible with the ICC model as they are the most collaborative and involving. They also provide immediate feedback for the members of the interview group and do some team building with them at the same time. Group interviews get participants sharing data and analyzing their importance very quickly and are thus a great way to start modeling the ICC method.

A further review of the data-collection methods in Figure 10 suggests how several of the methods can be combined to strengthen the usefulness of data collected from only one method. For example, adding interviews to the usual questionnaire increases depth and ownership. Adding a document and record analysis provides a historical perspective based on publicly available material. Of course checking whatever you have found through the formal data collection with your own experiences so far in the organization gives an outsider's perspective. Tuning into your feelings about your own experiences also helps you empathize with what others in the system are likely to be feeling. Combining any three methods or sources of data is called *triangulation* and is thought to be one of the best ways of increasing data credibility.

Method	Design	Depth	Flexibility	Quantification	Time to Do	Effects of Doing	Other
Interview	Easy	Much/most	Most	Difficult (content analysis)	Much	Builds trust, may change people's views	Open to bias
Group interview	Easy	Much	Much	Difficult	Medium	Strong on group building	Difficulty maintaining focus
Questionnaire	Difficult (preparation takes time)	Less (depends on length and complexity)	Less	Easy	Least	Less trust building—may change views	Objective and can cover many people
Observation	Varies (depends on how systematic)	More (can't deny behavior)	Varies	Varies (systematic tabulation easy, but narrative record hard)	Much	Possible problem if observers seen as intruders or evaluators	Do observers participate?
Records and documents	Easy	Varies	Least	Least	Some, but varies with complexity of records	Least (no effect)	Public data vs. real data
Projective (drawings, skits, collage, fantasy)	Easy	Varies	Most	Varies to difficult	Little	Range from great fun to threatening	May not be taken seriously
Your experience in the system	Happens anyway	Medium to much	Depends on what you do	Difficult	Little to none	Nothing more	Need to tune into your instincts

Figure 10. Methods of Data Collection

be involved in collecting and providing the data with what is practical, credible, and cost effective. In terms of collaboration it is great for everyone to interview one another and then summarize it together. However, when you have large numbers of people with no interviewing skills who don't trust one another enough to say anything of importance, whatever is collected would be suspect. It might be of little help in identifying the real issues and moving the intervention forward. There are a number of procedures that seek optimal levels of involvement through organization and structure and through training participants in data-collection skills. A few of the methods that are the best compromises of involvement with practicality are described in the next section.

Selected Procedures

1. SYSTEMS IMPROVEMENT RESEARCH

The Systems Improvement Research (SIR) model (Dimock, 1978, 1979, 1981) is based on a collaborative approach to data collection that joins the external consultants with the internal participants as a data-collection and analysis team. The team proposes the areas it wants studied or the questions it wants answered; using the consultants as special resources, the team prepares the data-collection tool (questionnaire, interview schedule, or observation guide). The team then divides up to collect the data, usually pairing an insider and an outsider (consultant) to conduct an interview, observe a meeting, or distribute a questionnaire. In some cases, the consultants may take on a training/coaching role in training the insiders in data-collection methods. But the primary reason for pairing an insider and outsider is to join the strength of the consultant's objective point of view and conceptual framework with the insider's understanding of group norms and ability to understand hidden meanings or subtle points in the data. Thus outside objectivity and perspective is coupled with the relevant biases and historical interpretations of the insider. Some respondents find it easier to talk to an insider while others prefer an outsider; pairing data collectors is a useful way of meeting some of both sets of needs.

The other important aspect of the SIR method, with relevance to data collection, is the powerful impact of immediate feedback of the data into the system. The immediate feedback capitalizes on the energy generated by the data-collection process and eliminates any possibility that the data can be discounted by labeling them stale or out of date. Often the immediate sharing of data facilitates a continuing discussion and exploration of the areas under study, which adds to the quality of the data available. This is a technique adopted from interview methods in which the interviewer summarizes the points of view of the respondent and usually finds that the summary generates further thinking and responses from the interviewee.

2. INTEREST CENSUS

The most basic group method of data collection is the interest census, in which people come together in their natural groups (preferably between five and sixty or eighty people) and are asked about their interests or problems related to the overall goals of the intervention. This process is usually facilitated by asking people at the opening of such a meeting to take a moment and list their interests. Sample questions include the following:

- What interests do you have that you think would increase the effectiveness of your work?

- What are the major issues in this community that we should give attention to in the next two years?

- List the ideas you have to deal with the budget cutbacks that have been thrust on us.

- What problems would you like to work on in the forthcoming intervention program?

- List the changes that would please you personally and also benefit the organization.

After people complete their lists, they are asked to form subgroups of five to seven people to explore the ideas of the participants, to brainstorm new interests, and finally to make up a list of high-priority items to share with the other groups. As each subgroup presents its three or four items of greatest importance, a master list is prepared (usually on flip-chart sheets taped to the wall).

When all the groups have reported, the consultant and the group summarize the items under appropriate headings or categories. These may be color coded or given a specific category title. When the categories are generally agreed on and a check is made that the input of all the participants shows up somewhere, the group establishes the top-priority categories for immediate consideration and possible action planning. The master list is reproduced and distributed to be used later as a checking point for progress.

3. SWOT ANALYSIS

The acronym SWOT stands for Strengths, Weaknesses, Opportunities, and Threats. It is an extension of the force-field analysis model described as the eighth assumption about changing social systems. Describing the present strengths and weaknesses of the internal system is preceded by describing the perceived opportunities and threats in the external system. It is harder to list the opportunities and threats to your community or agency from outside forces such as economic conditions and government regulations so it is done first. A systematic external and internal environmental scan provides a powerful framework within which to set goals and plan relevant actions.

A SWOT analysis clarifies the tensions that exist between the present performance of a system and its goals. This is done by contrasting two basic dimensions: good versus bad (strengths and opportunities with weaknesses and threats) and present versus future (strengths and weaknesses with opportunities and threats). The procedure used to do the SWOT analysis can be the same as the one used in the *Interest Census* described previously, with each of the four components a separate question and activity. Figure 11 illustrates a way to summarize the completed activity using the top three items for each of the four questions. This identifies the combinations most likely to produce results and what needs to be done to make the "consider" and "maybe" combinations possible.

Figure 11 puts the data collected from the SWOT analysis into perspective. It suggests the most likely activities for immediate success–the combination of strengths and opportunities that appears in the top, right-hand quadrant labeled "go." It also clarifies that the strengths listed in the "consider" quadrant have external restraints that are likely to reduce their success. These restraints (such as changes in government priorities, changes in consumer interests, or an economic downturn) are best handled by planning action strategies to reduce their impacts. The present weaknesses to implementing the opportunities found in the "maybe" quadrant may be overcome with additional personnel, equipment, or facilities. Or, as would be the case in a change in service delivery from individual treatment to group- and community-oriented prevention, the kind of staff needed might change, as would the locations and layouts for facilities.

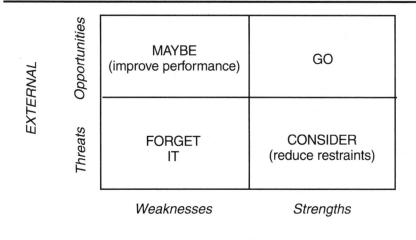

Figure 11. SWOT Summary

4. STAKEHOLDER ANALYSIS

The second most important assumption mentioned earlier about changing social systems was that those people affected by a change should be involved in making that change. This sounds great in the abstract, but who are these people and how might they be impacted by the program you are planning? A stakeholder is any person, group, or organization who has claim to (or serious interest in) the activities and well-being of the system targeted for change.

In a community, stakeholders include all full-time and part-time residents, all businesses and absentee landlords, related governing bodies, unions, and political parties. The stakeholders of a community-serving organization include present and former consumers of services, founders, employees' unions, boards (trustees), related governments, organizations providing parallel or complementary services, and suppliers of equipment and services.

The phases of a stakeholder analysis (Figure 12) are to identify and list the stakeholders, note their stake in the system's activities and well-being, predict the criteria they would use to assess the system's effectiveness, and then make an estimate of what their evaluation would be. If the focus is more specifically on the proposed intervention or development program, the last question would ask for an estimate of what their likely reaction to the project would be at this time.

A stakeholder analysis concludes with a review of the data focusing on the following factors:

1. Who are major stakeholders? The minor ones?

2. What is it they want from us (or what can we give them)?

3. How are they likely to evaluate our operation at this time?

4. How will they react to the proposed intervention or development program?

The final step asks for an action plan to head off or respond to key stakeholders' concerns, or to identify new ways to involve

Stakeholder (person, group, organization)	Give/Get	Likely evaluation of us now	Likely reaction to proposed development program
Taxpayers (residents)	Education, recreation, protection, & social services. [Country life style— moderate taxes.]	Good to very good. Want more services but no more taxes.	Mixed. Desire systematic plan. Want rural life but want to sever lots to sell. Don't want commerce or gravel or landfill near by.
Seasonal residents	Roads, recreation, & protection.	Very good. Love untaxed status.	Trailer-park seasonals want to stay all year and pay little or no tax. No sewerage upgrading.
Churches	Protection of property. [Opportunity to influence community well-being.]	Very good. Churches holding their own member-wise.	Freedom to expand retreat centers and graveyards. Insist on rural character. Against any development.

Note: Abridged sample of stakeholder analysis done by Town Council of rural community of Puslinch, Ontario, while planning a long-range program for land use in township.

Figure 12. Stakeholder Analysis

them in the planning process so that their stakes can receive consideration.

Analyzing a System's Culture

The focus of change using the ICC method is the culture of the system targeted for change. The culture of a system has been described as its usual ways of doing things and consists of norms or standards, values and beliefs, and the mythology and folklore built up over time. Culture is nebulous, hard to define, and is revealed like an onion, one layer at a time. Interveners, if they are new to the system, cannot understand the subtle meanings of the insiders' descriptions of culture–they are left with the surface layers. Also, insiders may not trust interveners with a whole picture even if they could describe it themselves. Often basic, usual ways of doing things are taken for granted and are difficult to think of as specific data.

The newcomer can usually uncover the first layer by observing the usual ways things happen in a place and contrasting it with other systems. Unusual norms or idiosyncrasies of the system are much more easily identified by the newcomer than the old-timer who takes it all for granted. As the intervener gains trust and acceptance from the insiders, they can work together to bring into consciousness the forgotten understandings of why the things that puzzle the intervener happen the way they do.

Group norms are statements of common and acceptable ways of doing things. People who have high status and acceptance in the system usually model these norms. For anyone investigating the culture of a system, these people (usually they are leaders) are worthy of systematic observation and study.

The Culture Analysis Questionnaire and Interview Guide (Figure 13) and the Observation Guide (Figure 14) will collect a great deal of information, especially if they are used for group participation. If the questionnaire approach seems the way to go, general meetings of stakeholders can be organized in which participants complete the questionnaire as individuals, then form groups of four to six people to analyze and summarize the results. As in the case of the Interest Census technique previously described, recorders/reporters from each group report the most significant findings to the total group. Although a complete list may be made of the work-group reports for careful study later, the most frequently identified significant findings are summarized for the total group. Perhaps too, the total group might wind up the

---

1. Your two best friends are joining this system tomorrow. What three things would you tell them they have to do to get ahead?

2. What would you tell them not to do in order to get ahead and gain acceptance?

3. List three adjectives (descriptive words) that are most descriptive of this system (community, group, or organization).

4. What are the three most prevalent behaviors of the leaders here?

5. What are the rituals and celebrations here? (How are new people introduced into the system, achievements celebrated, ghosts and failures buried?)

6. What activities here have the highest status?

7. What is the political culture of this system? What are the attitudes regarding mental and physical ability, sex, race, and religion? What about styles of power and control (autocratic, paternalistic, participative) or political orientation (radical, posturing liberal, conservative, reactionary)?

8. Culture is embedded in history, so it is helpful to know the folklore and history related to your system. Acceptance of this folklore often blocks change projects. Who were the good guys and the bad guys, the winners and the losers, and what is the folklore about what they did? What were the outcomes of previous change projects?

Figure 13. Culture Analysis of a Community, Group, or Organization: Questionnaire and Interview Guide

The goal is to identify the unwritten rules that determine the usual ways in which things work in this community, group, or organization.

- What behavior or activity gets rewarded? What gets demerits?
- What are the major sources of anxiety and concern?
- What are the norms for dress? Promptness? Attendance? Performance? Deadlines?
- What are the practices for handling routines, lateness, deadlines, absences, and poor performance?
- What are expectations for people to participate in and contribute to the system's well-being? ☐ High ☐ Medium ☐ Low
- What amount of support and encouragement is given to people here? ☐ High ☐ Medium ☐ Low
- How much openness/secrecy exists regarding: income level, competence, performance, promotions or awards, and future plans?
- What's talked about privately that isn't addressed publicly?
- How is unacceptable behavior punished (sarcasm, freezing out, whispering, confrontation, rejection)?
- How are people gotten rid of here?
- How is conflict, aggressive competition, and major disagreement handled?
- How is space used to symbolize status and power, to maintain privacy, to identify subgroups?
- How does the system deal with the external environment—the larger community of which it is part?
  1. Reactive (system lets itself be controlled)
  2. Proactive (system tries to control its destiny)
  3. Harmonizing (system interacts to work out mutually beneficial results)
- What appear to be the common hidden agendas of the system's culture?
- The three biggest culture supports of the system's goals and well-being are:
- The three biggest culture restraints to goal achievement and well-being are:

Figure 14. Culture-Analysis Observation Guide

session by discussing why these findings are the most important and what they are really saying about the system's culture.

If the questionnaire is to be used as an interview guide, participation and ownership of the data can be optimized by using the group interview technique (interviews with three to six people together). Or teams of interviewers, perhaps working in pairs, can do the interviews and then get together to discuss and summarize the learnings using the format of the general meeting described for the questionnaire. And lastly, if the number of identified stakeholders is less than one hundred, each stakeholder can interview a partner and then have the general meeting with small groups to discuss and summarize the information.

Similar procedures for maximizing participation can be used with the observation guide, forming a large team of observers or having everyone observe for a week and then convening a general meeting. Alternatively, pairs of observers can be formed using the Systems Improvement Research method with one insider paired with one outsider, or an old-timer paired with a newcomer.

Process Goals in Data Collection

Involving the people of the identified system in the process of collecting and analyzing data increases their commitment to the change program. But the process of interviewing people or framing questionnaires and discussing the findings with others is also a very powerful educational experience. Participants learn new ways of looking at the problem and may change some of their own attitudes and beliefs. And, best of all, because attitudes are sustained by the culture of the groups to which a person belongs, the discussions with the group can lead to modifications of its culture. The effective re-education of an individual requires shifts in the norms of closely related groups.

These insights formed the original concept of action research, which integrated personal re-education and social change into the same process. Changes in the usual ways of doing things came about as the stakeholder in the problem worked in a cooperative action-research method to study the problem and started trying out new ways of working. For example, if the identified problem was the low status of women in the community or organization and their inability to be heard and taken seriously by men, we can contrast two approaches to illustrate action research. First, let's look at the usual research approach that believes that accurate information will change males' attitudes and behavior toward women. Women would interview other women in the system about their experiences, especially in the system under study; women would do the interviews because women talk differently to other women than they do to men and would be more likely to reveal personal experiences and thus make the data collected more credible.

The action-research approach would start working on the problem as part of the data-collection process, believing that changes in attitudes and behavior come about through experiential activities focusing on group norms. Both men and women would interview women and then compare and contrast the results. General meetings would convene to discuss the results and the differences. Small groups formed separately of men and women would start the analysis at the general meeting; the groups then would re-form with both men and women to compare notes. All would be working together to understand the role and status of women and trying to figure out what was supporting and restraining present practices. In the process, women would be talking to men about real issues, and the men would be working at understanding their input in new ways. Roles and relationships—and the norms supporting present practices—would change as action-research activities put the new attitudes and ways of working into practice.

Participative Data Analysis and Reporting

There may be programs in which the intervener feels it would not be practical for the stakeholders to be involved in the collection of the necessary data. Or, existing data may be motivation for the program, such as in the case of a recent census showing a rapid growth trend for the community. But as the program moves into analyzing the meaning of the new information and informing others about it, it is imperative that participation be optimized, or the collaboration component of the ICC method will be lost.

The intervener or intervention team will likely do an analysis of the information collected because an outside perspective is usually helpful. Most analysis, however, will be done by individual consumers, study groups, and community meetings called for that purpose. Stakeholders will report their findings to one another with the intervener facilitating the process. In no way will the consultant lay out an analysis of the data with a diagnosis of the problem. Rather the analysis and suggestion of related factors will be done by the program participants.

The usual data-analysis procedures consist of the participants' summarizing the data and then looking for themes among them. Usually it is helpful to put the data into categories or at least clusters of similar information. With my bias for the force-field analysis technique, data would be divided into helping and hindering factors, strengths and weaknesses, pros and cons, or winners and losers. Following this division of the data, the participants would examine the two halves looking for general characteristics that were true for one half but not the other. Once these characteristic differences between the halves were identified, the group would hypothesize any generalizable principles to account for the differences. And lastly, analysis procedures would seek to establish the consistency and confirmability of the data by the triangulation method. Data from three different sources would be looked for to establish the credibility of any major theme. (These analysis procedures are described more fully in Dimock, 1987b.)

Goal Setting

The goal-setting phase of the intervention consists of reviewing the information forthcoming from the data-collection process, identifying and exploring possible goals, and setting priorities of clear, specific goals. Goal setting is the launching pad for thoughtful and manageable action planning–it needs to be solidly in place before the action planning can begin. Most planning groups find it very difficult to separate goal setting from action planning because examining the feasibility or practicability of implementing the goals helps to determine whether or not the goal is attainable. And if the goal is really not attainable, why then select it as a priority?

The information coming from an Interest or Problem Census or a SWOT analysis moves a group quickly to exploring the issues that have been identified and framing then into goals. Often this framing means changing the problem statement from a solution to an identification of the problem or interest. Thus, "getting more government funding for our community" may become "expanding our programs and services without increasing taxes." The latter framing suggests that present monies may be redistributed, cost-cutting efficiencies may be found and implemented, or a variety of sources of new, outside funding may be explored. Often half of the problems surfacing from an Interest Census are in fact suggested solutions and need to be reworked to clarify the goal.

Brainstorming

Probably the most useful technique to promote creative thinking and to free up and surface dreams and visions is brainstorming. Stakeholders, usually in a group, are asked to think of all the possible goals coming out of the data. As the ideas are called out by the participants, the facilitator lists them on newsprint or on overhead transparency so everyone can see them. The essential rule is that no evaluation or reaction to the ideas is permissable. In this way, very creative ideas often emerge as inhibitions are freed and participants mention possibly crazy or unrealistic ideas. Participants are simulated by the ideas of others and a different level of thinking takes place. Brainstorming's non-evaluative climate clearly separates the generation of ideas from the assessment of their feasibility and general worth.

Goal Evaluation

During the goal-evaluation process the focus is to make suggested goals clear, specific, and measurable. Thus a vague goal such as "to improve people's health" would be sharpened to read "to establish sound physical health practices with children and youth." It would be made more specific and measurable by adding "to provide a routine and expectations for at least thirty minutes of exercise three times a week."

Further evaluation of the goals would compare their strengths and weaknesses through a force-field analysis or the pro-con technique. The force field has been described on pp. 27 through 29, and the pro-con asks stakeholders to list everything in favor of a course of action and then to list everything against it. When long lists of factors are identified they can be ranked or rated on their importance. The method I most frequently use is to give everyone three votes for the most important strengths and three for the most important weaknesses. This has the effect of giving a rapid and manageable ranking of the items that is quite reliable.

Setting Priorities

Selecting goals for action planning and implementation is a process of setting priorities rather than discarding many of the goals. It may be that low-priority goals this year will change in importance and be high-priority goals another time. The important considerations in selection are desirability, feasibility, and likely outcome.

By desirability I mean the value or importance that would be placed on the change. For example, in a rural community would it be more important to provide uncontaminated drinking water, to educate mothers on nutritional requirements of newborn children, or to introduce more effective farming practices?

Looking at the feasibility, it's clear that two or three community wells could provide adequate water; if the means of digging or drilling and maintaining them were available, they would be very feasible. Educating mothers on nutritional needs might be feasible if the educational programs or health educators were available and foods or diet supplements required for the newborn children could be found at low cost. The modification of farming practices with the introduction of new methods would require a change in the usual way of doing things, a difficult accomplishment at best. It might also require new seed, fertilizer, equipment, or land drainage or irrigation.

The likely outcomes are a combination of the sustaining forces for the new activities versus the restraining forces or risks involved. Predicting the probability of an outcome is a mutually exclusive process. Only one outcome is possible. That is why the percentages you give to the best possible outcome and the worst possible outcome should add up to one hundred. This is not to suggest that risky goals should be eliminated but rather that it should be an informed decision-making process. Perhaps the major difference between doing something foolhardy and something courageous is making the decision on the basis of thoughtful consideration of risks and possibilities.

The final choice of priorities can be assisted through the use of ranking, rating, or weighting techniques. Ranking asks the stakeholders to list their goals in order of preference considering desirability, feasibility, and likely outcome. The choices are collated and the average rank for each goal established and reported back. The three-votes method described previously is a short form of this method. Rating asks stakeholders to give a preference to each goal on a scale, such as "1" means very important, "2" means fairly important, and "3" means not too important. The results are collated showing average ratings and reported to the stakeholders. The weighting technique asks participants to assume that they have ten units that they can assign to the suggested goals, depending on their perceived preference. All units can be given to one goal or they can be divided into preferences for up to ten goals (no partial unit allocations allowed). The results are summarized showing group averages and presented to the stakeholders for their final choices of priorities.

All of these priority-setting techniques are very scientific and objective. My experience suggests that although these techniques are often helpful there is another element that I call "political reality" that can easily be the real basis for selection. Interveners should not be discouraged by these politically based choices of priorities but try to be up-front themselves and help the stakeholders be up-front about the basis of their goal choices.

Action Planning

The action-planning phase of an intervention consists of laying out the specific procedures or activities that will most likely achieve the agreed-on priority goals. These plans will describe who is doing what, when, where, and requiring what resources. This detailed planning is often turned over to a planning or steering committee to be worked out. When the proposed plans are completed–there is often more than one approach to the achievement of the goal–they are presented to the stakeholders for modification and ratification.

It is vital that the final plan describe objectives and activities that can be monitored as the implementation starts. This includes a very clear time line (what is supposed to happen when) and intended outcomes along this time line. Figures 15 and 16 show the layout of a typical project for a human-service organization and examples of project success indicators are shown in the program-evaluation chapter. It is important to involve the stakeholders extensively at this phase, especially if a steering committee has done the work. Sessions involving the stakeholders can be built around the following design:

1. Introduction of the plans and the rationale for them.

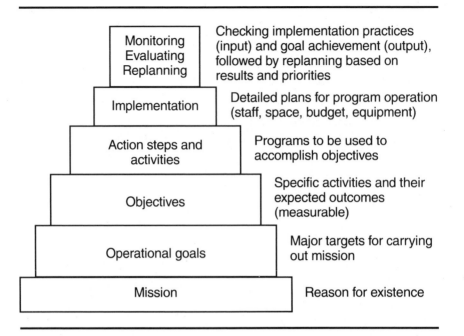

Figure 15. Outline for an Organization Revitalization Intervention

2. Clarification-oriented questions and discussion of the plans (very brief).

3. Brainstorming a list of the strengths of the plans.

4. Brainstorming a list of the weaknesses of the plans.

5. Brainstorming suggestions to improve the plans either by building on their strengths or especially by reducing the impact of their weaknesses.

6. Arranging for next steps to brush up the plans and start their implementation.

It is assumed that the lists would be analyzed by the steering committee and used to make appropriate modifications in the plans. If serious resistance to the plans surfaces, another round of consideration might be worthwhile to increase stakeholder commitment and the credibility of the plans.

YM-YWCA Example

Mission: The development of well-rounded, self-actualized individuals.

Goals: To establish sound physical-health practices with children and youth.

Objective: To provide a routine and expectations for at least thirty minutes of exercise, three times a week.
To provide an understanding of basic minimum nutritional requirements.

Action Steps: To initiate and operate five physical-health programs for children and youth (6-16) in decentralized areas.

(Standards)

- in each of eight major areas of the city.
- for a minimum of fifteen participants per location participating two or three times a week.
- within the next six months.
- at a cost of $3,000 per location per year.

Implementation: Show a plan for staff and volunteer operation of the eight programs and how the programs will be assessed. Show a plan for budget, equipment, rental space needed for implementation.

Monitoring & Evaluating: Were the eight programs set up with the planned quality and focus of the program?

Replanning: How much progress did the participants make toward the stated objectives of the program? Are any hard data available on objectives of exercise and nutrition? What should be the next steps in replanning this program? And what should be its place in overall Y priorities?

Figure 16. Sample Revitalization Planning Intervention

The major features of the action-planning phase of the ICC model start with who is to do what, when, and where and necessary resources. Following these basics, special attention is given to such questions as:

- How can we effectively involve the stakeholder in this action-planning phase?
- How can we reduce the resistance or restraining features of the action plan?
- Who are the appropriate people to champion the implementation of various parts of the plans (people who will lead and be responsible for the activities)?

Another consideration is dealing with the fifth assumption about changing social systems, namely that change in one part of a system will produce strain in related parts and require changes in them. This means figuring out who the people or subgroups in this system or in related systems are that will be impacted by the plans over time and establishing some contingency strategies to deal with them.

The final consideration of the action-planning stage relates to the usual lull or slowdown of momentum that takes place shortly after implementation has started. This is the point at which interventions most frequently break down. It is a challenge to keep the stakeholders involved during early implementation, and the new ways of doing things take a while to catch on. Or to put it differently, identifying needs, collecting and analyzing data, and goal setting and action planning are intellectual activities that are fun. Implementing action plans requires new behavior that is stressful and perhaps unpleasant. Ideas are common, as I say; it's the implementation that counts.

Definite procedures with realistic time frames to monitor the "doing" phase should be incorporated into the action planning with provisions to modify the plans if they are not meeting expectations or to switch to an alternative backup plan. And if they are meeting expectations, celebrations involving all the stakeholders have been incorporated into the action plan.

Action Taking

As was just mentioned, the challenge of the implementation phase of an intervention is to maintain stakeholder interest and enthusiasm after the excitement of the planning process concludes. It is especially challenging to deal with the resistance that can be expected when participants try to change their behaviors to establish the new ways of doing things.

In an ICC intervention, as many of the stakeholders as possible are involved in action-taking activities. Special activities may be set up to involve key stakeholders who have other responsibilities that prevent their ongoing participation. For example, in a school board project introducing student-centered, experiential learning into a high school, senior administration and school board trustees were identified as key stakeholders. They were invited to the demonstration classrooms to work for a session as assistant leaders or classroom observers. The observers were given the observation guide to complete that was part of the program's evaluation. In both cases the invited stakeholders participated in the regular staff planning and debriefing for that session. When the students planned a weekend retreat, other key stakeholders were invited to come and lead segments of the program.

"Resistance to change is normal and helpful in stabilizing new changes" is Assumption 7 about changing social systems. Likely resistance was considered in the planning stage and hopefully specific plans were created to reduce the impact of restraining forces. It is important to follow through with these plans during the action-taking phase. The best way to deal with resistance is to get it out in the open, talk about it, and try to understand it for what it is. A usual approach that fits in well with the monitoring dimension of the action-taking phase is the periodic checkup meeting. The first of these meetings of participants is scheduled to take place before serious resistance surfaces. At these meetings the progress of the intervention as seen by the participants is assessed. Possible or likely resistance taking place is identified and discussed. The meeting facilitator might ask questions such as the following:

- If there were resistance to our implementation activities at this time, what form would it likely take?
- What is our best guess about the cause of this resistance?

How can we help each other to make the resistance easier to handle?

In such a meeting no person or subgroup is put on the spot. Resistance to change is considered a normal, healthy response. The group discussion helps to clarify the newly expected standards of behavior and to support participants in the change process while gently pressuring the deviants to live up to the expectations of their friends and colleagues.

The intervention participants joined this project because they wanted to see some good things happen and because they wanted to be part of the action. It is important that the periodic monitoring reviews and celebrations proclaim the progress of the intervention toward its goals. The goal-achievement review is most helpful if it shows each person contributed to the success of the group. The more widely a project's achievements are known, the more partici-pants can bask in its reflected glory. Increasing the status and recognition of the project participants in the community is a sure way, too, of raising their enthusiasm for being part of the action. And, the more attractive the project, the more likely they will work at changing their usual ways of doing things to meet the new goals.

Evaluation and Replanning

The specific, measurable objectives of the project were spelled out in the goal-setting and action-planning stages of the inter-vention. The action-planning time line gave dates for the moni-toring reviews and the more complete program review. One year after the start of the action-taking phase would be the maximum for this complete review activity, and my experience suggests that six to nine months is the more appropriate time frame.

In addition to assessing the measurable objectives and other program achievement indicators, it may be beneficial to redo some of the early data-collection procedures for comparison and to aid in replanning. These procedures would most likely include (if they had been done previously) the interest census, the SWOT analysis, and the stakeholder analysis. The culture analysis might also be included if done before, but its more nebulous data make it more difficult to use in replanning. The more previous data-collection methods–now serving as evaluation methods by comparing the results with previous results–are used, the more likely stakeholders will see the results as confirmable and credible.

The rule of thumb for the amount of time and energy to be devoted to this phase is one third to one half that given to the original data-collection, goal-setting, and action-planning activities. This may seem excessive, yet there is a vital new learning here that is essential to the success of an ICC project. That is, how can we use our own experiences to plan for the future success and effectiveness of our community, group, or organization?

Establishing Closure

It would be great to imagine that interventions come naturally to a close when the stakeholders have learned how to use their experience to plan for the future success and effectiveness of their community and have empowered themselves sufficiently and developed problem-solving skills that enable them to run the project themselves. In reality, interventions include estimates of the length of time needed to achieve the goals. Or in the case of many community-development projects, the sponsoring agency may set an arbitrary time span into which projects are expected to fit. Projects with the Canadian University Service Overseas and the Canadian International Development Agency typically have two-year time spans. Closure is the point at which the intervener or intervention team leave the project, and it should be planned for carefully.

Leaving the project too early may create a feeling among the participants of being deserted. Such a feeling could lead to demoralization of the stakeholders and perhaps a readiness to get even by stopping work on the project altogether. Staying too long on a project can create dependency and reduce the ability of the participants to empower themselves and take over project leadership. But if the budget has run out or the assignment is over, closure should be made as comfortable and empowering for the stakeholders as possible.

My bias is to negotiate the time and style of closure with the system. In many of our Centre interventions, we build in one or two specific dates to negotiate whether we will continue and if so what our focus will be. In organizations there are "change-of-scope" meetings and in communities there are regular review sessions. Many interventions just peter out as there is no closure. This may leave participants wondering why the intervention stopped and whether that represents success or failure. The uneasy feeling about the ending of this intervention becomes part of the folklore and may impede future interventions.

At a minimum the closure activity should include a review and discussion of what the intervention did and did not accomplish as well as a discussion of the intervention process–how the intervener(s) and stakeholders worked together. A consideration of where the project goes from here is a third useful activity. Finally, the project closure needs to be communicated to all the stakeholders, especially those in related systems not connected to the regular grapevine. Some kind of a final report may surface after an intervention is over, but it is my bias that it should not be considered part of the closure activity. These reports usually come out too long after the project is over to be of much use to the stakeholders and they do not provide an opportunity for participants to deal with their feelings about the project.

The following are some other specific ideas to help you plan closure activities:

1. Review evaluation data and discuss perceptions of them. This could include discussing some of the learnings in the process.

2. Go around the group or at least discuss the questions of "What was the most important part of this experience for me?" and "What am I most concerned about now that it is over?"

3. Have small groups review the whole intervention and make lists of what they thought helped the intervention and what hindered it. These lists would then be reported back to the total group.

4. A small committee would prepare a working paper for the total group on its perspective of the social intervention, with special focus on the present state of affairs. A force-field analysis could be used to show where things were at the beginning of the intervention and where they are now. This would help focus on how stable the changes were likely to be.

5. The group has a guided imagery about what is going to happen (for themselves personally or for the social system) now that the intervention is over. The group could imagine that the intervention is just starting and talk about what they imagine is going to happen. This is another way of evaluating what did happen, but does not blame or reward anyone. It helps to focus on the group's taking responsibility for what could happen in future dealings with change activities.

6. A brief presentation is made on typical ways of dealing with termination followed by going around the group and reporting "here-and-now" feelings about closure.

7. Material from an early stage is presented and small groups work up and report on what is happening differently now. This early material could be a tape recording or videotape of an early session, the record of a meeting, a list of early goals and objectives, or some kind of a working document or data-collection summary typical of that phase of the intervention.

8. If the group is not available for a closure activity, a report on the intervention (perhaps only two or three pages) is prepared by the intervener(s) or a committee and sent to each participant.

9. If the intervention ends abruptly or peters out, the intervener writes a letter to everyone about the ending or lack of closure and invites responses.

Closure is a wonderful opportunity to celebrate and have fun. A potluck picnic or supper (in the collaborative style of the intervention) is a popular choice. Or add to the regular review meeting planned for closure a recognition period, a sing-along, dance, or informal skit presentations. Prayers or some kind of a worship service may be effective in some communities.

Part Six

Evaluating Interventions

A foremost attraction of the ICC method of organizing change programs is that it has a built-in program evaluation. In fact, ICC is an intervention-evaluation method. It starts by collecting facts about the present status of the system targeted for change— usually from three or more sources or perspectives. The facts are analyzed and used to establish goals for the intervention. In the action-planning stage, measurable objectives are described with expected outcomes within various time periods. Action taking builds in regular reviews of progress, often using the same data-collection methods used the first time. Thus, at any point in time, and certainly by closure, there is comparable data from at least three sources on system changes related to the intervention. The three data sources provide an opportunity to triangulate the data, a procedure that gives credibility and conformability to any noticed results of the intervention assuring they are accurate and real.

In textbooks on program evaluation, this ICC approach is called the *continuous-monitoring* method. This method is more accurate in its reporting than some others as it collects impact assessments from more than one or two points in time. Interventions are like the stock market, up and down all the time; the more these ups and downs can be recorded, the more complete the picture of the intervention and its effects is likely to be.

Let me now put this continuous-monitoring method of intervention evaluation into perspective (Figure 17). Hopefully this will encourage the reader to use the ICC model because of these great evaluation strengths. And for those interventions not able to use the ICC model, some very useful alternatives will be suggested.

Level	Type	Answers this question:
LOW	INPUT	What time, resources, and activities went into the intervention?
LOW	REACTION	How satisfied were the stakeholders with the program?
MEDIUM	LEARNING	What did the participants learn in the program?
HIGH	BEHAVIOR	How did participants change their behavior based on what they learned?
TOP	RESULTS	How useful were the results of these new behaviors?

Figure 17. Intervention Evaluation

Levels of Evaluation

An *input* evaluation looks at what was put into the intervention, both quantity and quality. For example, an input study of the Toronto Blue Jays baseball team would show the hours spent in training and the focus of the training (batting, fielding, base running, and so on) and describe the participation of the coaching staff. It might describe the "power" meals that the team ate and the nutritional qualities of those meals. It might also record the average hours of sleep members had each night or the relaxing activities and atmosphere of the training location. Most input evaluations in the human services that I read describe the academic qualifications of the staff and their years of experience. Interesting information perhaps but nothing that would satisfy a Jays fan who wants to know if the team is winning its games. Results are the name of this game with everything riding on wins and losses, runs scored per game by Jays and opponents, individual batting averages, base running, fielding, and injury comparisons. Above all, fans want to know if the team's performance is improving and whether or not it has a chance at the pennant.

A *reaction* evaluation is typical of most group and organization interventions especially those of a team-building, group-revitalization, or training nature. I call this the "happiness scale." Although I agree that happy participants are more likely to rehire the consultant, the assumption that happiness is a direct indicator of behavior change and organization improvement is a bit thin.

Learning is the first step toward change; but all learning, especially the acquisition of new knowledge, does not lead to changes in behavior. Everyone knows people who have all the knowledge but don't practice what they preach. It is necessary to follow up on the stakeholders' securing of new information and insights and to determine what kind of behavior change took place. It is like taking the graduates of a course in leadership who have had their learnings evaluated by a final examination grade and following up on them for a month to find out the extent to which the graduates put the new learnings into practice.

The *results* evaluation assesses the impact of the behavior change on the targeted system. This is especially important in interventions in which the goal is a change in the culture as it is more than and different from the sum of individual behavior changes. During the 1960s I was heavily involved in the Human Relations Training movement. In the early years our evaluations measured learnings and attitude changes of participants. We were delighted to find participants learned a great deal about themselves and their relationships with others. They became less authoritarian, dogmatic, and prejudiced, and more cooperative and participative in their leadership style. Quite a few years later we started *results* evaluations and found over 5 percent of participants deciding to plan a new life style that included a career change. Other participants returned to work and gave their managers feedback about how they really thought things were going on the job. Others wanted to humanize the workplace; teachers introduced developmental discussions into their classrooms, and ministers opened their sermons into dialogues with the congregation. Our participants were seen by their colleagues as being open and personable but perhaps flaky and less concerned about getting the job done. Clearly there were more results with sensitivity training than any other kind of training, but it was difficult to decide which changes were helpful. The behavior change and results were consistent with the self-actualizing objectives of the training but in many cases were seen as counterproductive by the employer stakeholders (to say nothing of many spouses or partners). So in addition to knowing the Jays have had 21 wins and 8 losses, the concerned stakeholder (avid fan) would want to know where the team stood in the league and what its chances were for getting into the World Series.

Some program evaluators might feel that if you do a thorough *results* assessment you don't need the other methods. All of the methods are typically included in the ICC model for two reasons. First, they provide information necessary to the goal-setting process; second, it is helpful to know which parts of the intervention are having the greatest impacts—a cost-effectiveness consideration. Figure 18 compares the various evaluation methods and puts them into perspective.

A review of the ICC data-collection methods in the perspective of Figure 18 shows that they all fit well into the continuous-monitoring style, and all of them focus on outcomes and results. The *Interest Census*, which may have been done as a needs-assessment or problem census, will show the extent to which stakeholders perceive their interests being met though the intervention. The same is true of the give/get technique described in the entry phase. For example, residents of the Cree community in Mistassini, Quebec, list housing (most are living year round in tents) and education as their top two problems. When a problem census is done again six months and eighteen months later and they are still the top two concerns, the outcome is that stakeholders still see them as the major concerns. When the third top concern of

Sample:

Input ⟶ Intervention ⟶ Output ⟶ Results

1. NEEDS ASSESSMENT (INTEREST CENSUS). What needs to be done.
   |· ·|

2. EFFORT EVALUATION. Input of time, energy, resources.
   |————————|

3. PROCESS EVALUATION. How things were done and how participants reacted.
   |————————————|

4. PROGRAM EFFECTIVENESS. Learnings, skills, attitudes.
   |————————————————————|

5. CONTINUOUS MONITORING. ICC and SIR model.
   |· · · / · · · / · · · / · · · / · · · / · · · / · · · / · · |

6. OUTCOME EVALUATION. Behavior change and measurable objectives.
   |————————————————|

7. RESULTS EVALUATION. Impact assessment.
   |——————————————————————|

Figure 18. Evaluating Interventions

the first census, involvement in local decision making, disappears from the second and third census, the outcome is the stakeholders no longer feel it is a problem. As an intervention progresses, the problems change and different problems arise.

The *culture analysis* works in much the same way, especially the questionnaire or interview format whereby the results are more easily quantifiable than with observations. The outcome of intervention activity will show up as changes in participants' perceptions of their culture. The SWOT *summary, stakeholder analysis,* and *environmental scans* all provide credible and confirmable qualitative measures of an intervention's outcome and results.

Consider a university that wants to increase the involvement and donations of its alumni. A stakeholder analysis starts with an alumni questionnaire recording attitudes, satisfaction, and involvement related to the university and its activities. A repeat questionnaire to the same sample of hundreds of alumni eighteen months later has different results. Attitudes toward the university are much more positive, and alumni are much more interested in participating in university activities. These data are supported by a 22 percent increase in registrations at university events (homecoming, short courses, regional meetings), by a 17 percent increase in total donations, and by a 10 percent increase in the number of people donating—quite credible measures of the outcomes and results of the interventions.

Measurable Objectives

In the goal-setting and action-planning phases, I described the role of *measurable objectives.* These are specific activities and their expected outcomes are measurable. Figures 15 and 16 (pages 66 and 67) showed an example of how this was done. Measurable objectives are usually the best approach to program evaluation as they are specific to that project. Inasmuch as they were established during the goal-setting and action-planning activities by the stakeholders and monitored during the action-taking duration of the intervention, they meet all the criteria of the ICC continuous-monitoring method of program evaluation.

The field-study example used in Figure 19 shows an organization that after many years of centralized programs focused on training, conferences, and educational materials decided to try an outreach project into the local communities. The method was to hire local field consultants to work with the local coordinating committees hoping to strengthen the committees and expand their influence in the community. This new field-consultant program also represented a shift in service-delivery focus from experts doing training and providing technical educational material for people working in the field to a community-development focus hoping to influence local cultures or usual ways of doing things. Evaluating the effectiveness of this new approach was a high priority for the

---

Center for the Prevention of Child Abuse

Mission of Center: To prevent all forms of child abuse.

Core Values: • commitment to Center philosophy
• commitment to building on local strengths.

Goal of Field-Consultant Program: To promote child-abuse prevention at the local level through support of local child-abuse coordinating committees.

Strategies to Reach Goal:

1. Regular consultations with local child-abuse committees through phone, mail, and on-site visits.

2. Providing and facilitating networking opportunities.

3. Regular feedback to the Center about committees, progress, programs, activities, and needs.

4. Field-consultant participation at regular training programs provided by the Center.

Measurable Indicators

How are we doing?
• Satisfaction and growth as field consultants;
• Completion of our own goals and long-range plans;
• Change in Field Consultant role from initiator to resource;
• Evaluation by our local coordinating committees; and
• Evaluation by the Center.

Figure 19. Field-Study Example (continued on page 82)

How are our local Child-Abuse Committees doing?

- Strength/satisfaction of Committees measured by attendance (turn-over), networking, and activities;
- Change in structure (more community input rather than all professional);
- Measurement of their own impact within communities (who knows of them?);
- Assessment of their own goals;
- Move toward more prevention and advocacy;
- Increase in use of Center resources;
- Increase in number of active local committees; and
- Increased number of local committee members at conference and other Center events and at regional meetings.

How is the Center doing?

- Field Consultants still in place;
- Local committees take on larger role in primary prevention;
- Reduction in child-abuse statistics;
- Wider representation from community on local committees;
- Increased feedback between local child-abuse committees and the Center through the Field Consultants;
- More awareness of local needs in order to develop programs materials; and
- Increased profile for Center as a resource (and requests of these resources).

How is the Babysitting Project doing?

- Number of courses;
- Number of communities involved;
- Increase in number of boys attracted to course;
- Decrease in statistics showing babysitters as abusers;
- Increased use of babysitting course as a prevention tool;
- Increased opportunity for local committees to make community links;
- Expansion of local committee mandates to encompass all children; and
- Use of babysitting course or materials by schools or other agencies.

Figure 19 (continued). Field-Study Example

Center. After a year's experience, the thirteen field consultants prepared the list of measurable indicators in one of their training sessions using the brainstorming technique; these are also shown in Figure 19.

The following three additional program evaluation tools also were developed to follow up on three of the important measurable indicator areas.

1. How well are the local committees doing (and are the field consultants helping them work more effectively)? Coordinating-Committee Evaluation, Figure 20.

2. How are the field consultants doing? Evaluation of their work by local committees. Center Planning Questionnaire, Figure 21.

3. Field consultants facilitate a regional conference once a year and increase participation in it. Field Consultant Sample Action Plan, Figure 22.

PURPOSE: (Clarity and agreement of purpose and priorities)

What do you think are the goals of this coordinating committee?

1. _____

2. _____

3. _____

How clear are these goals to you? ☐ Not clear ☐ Fuzzy ☐ Clear
How clear to other members? ☐ Not clear ☐ Fuzzy ☐ Clear
What are your top three action priorities for the next three months?

1. _____

2. _____

3. _____

ROLES: (Clarity and agreement of roles and responsibilities)

How clear are you about your role and responsibility in this committee?
☐ Not clear ☐ Fuzzy ☐ Clear
How clear are other members about their roles and responsibilities?
☐ Not clear ☐ Fuzzy ☐ Clear

PROCEDURES: (Clarity about how committee will work)

How clear are procedures for making decisions?
☐ Not clear ☐ Fuzzy ☐ Clear
How clear are procedures for solving problems?
☐ Not clear ☐ Fuzzy ☐ Clear
How clear are procedures for setting priorities?
☐ Not clear ☐ Fuzzy ☐ Clear

INTERPERSONAL RELATIONS: (Degree of trust, support, and respect)

How much do members trust one another?
☐ Little ☐ Some ☐ A lot
How much do members support one another?
☐ Little ☐ Some ☐ A lot
How much do members respect one another?
☐ Little ☐ Some ☐ A lot

Figure 20. Coordinating-Committee Evaluation

Child-Abuse Coordinating Council City/Region _____

YOUR NAME _____

The Center for the Prevention of Child Abuse would like to get your assessment of its activities and resources to help in future planning. Would you rate the importance to you of the Center activities below by showing how you would allocate ten dollars (0 to 10 dollars per item).

1. Hands-on materials such as the Babysitting Package. _____

2. Back-up and technical resources (films, books, pamphlets on child abuse). _____

3. Direct support from Field Consultants. _____

4. Funding to assist Coordinating Committee in its work. _____

5. Education and training for Coordinating Committee members (national conference, interdisciplinary training). _____

6. Advocacy for regional activities about child abuse. _____

TOTAL = __$10__

To help us understand your weighting of the importance of the above activities please tell us the following:

1. Number of people on your coordinating committee? _____

2. How many times has the committee met in the past 12 months? _____

3. For how many years have you been a committee member? _____

4. Are you familiar with the Center Babysitting Package entitled *Can You Babysit Tonight?* ☐ No ☐ Yes

5. Does your coordinating committee have any plans to make use of the Babysitting Package? ☐ Don't know ☐ No ☐ Yes

6. List the Center conferences and training programs you have attended, if any. _____

7. Please describe your contact, if any, with your Field Consultant?

_____

8. How helpful has the work of your Field Consultant been? (circle one)
   Little   A bit   Some   A lot   A great deal

9. How much impact do you think your Coordinating Committee has had in your community?
   Little   A bit   Some   A lot   A great deal

10. How well is your Coordinating Committee known by the human services in your community (police, school board, children's programs)?
   Little   A bit   Some   A lot   A great deal

Figure 21. Center Planning Questionnaire

Date _____

Field Consultant Action Plan

1. *GOAL:* To have a regional meeting.

2. *OBJECTIVE* (including measurable outcomes):
   Have all five coordinating committees, represented by at least three participants, at a regional meeting of a half-day or more. The content of the meeting to be sharing their activities and concerns and identifying issues for regional collaboration.

3. *ACTION PLAN:*
   • I'll seed the regional meeting idea with all five coordinating committees in my area.
   • I'll ask that it be put on the agenda of a forthcoming meeting.
   • I'll attend the meeting and speak to the idea or brief the chair to speak to it.
   • Ask for one member for a regional committee to plan it.
   • Meet with these five planners and facilitate and serve as a resource for their planning—will act as chair if needed.

4. *TIME LINE:*
   Seeding January-March; planning committee for regional meeting April and May; regional meeting in early October (and drum up participants for Center conference October 21-23).

5. *YOUR TIME NEEDED FOR THIS PLAN:*
   Five hours for seeding; ten hours for meetings or briefings; six for planning committee and follow-up; eight hours for preparation and follow-up of regional meeting.

   TOTAL 2 to 2½ days

Figure 22. Field Consultant Sample Action Plan

Organizing and Leading Interventions

In addition to guiding the planning and implementation of an intervention, the intervener is responsible for its leadership. This means the intervener provides the vision for the project, builds internal collaboration, develops trust and openness, and models the new ways of doing things. The intervener also is responsible for the recruitment and operation of the steering committee or intervention team. And the intervener is accountable for the training, coaching, and personal development of the key stakeholders. Some of the activities related to these responsibilities will be taken on by others as part of the empowerment process, but the responsibility stops with the intervener.

The position of the intervener as the facilitator of the desired change program gives him or her a very visible role in helping stakeholders see and feel the vision for the future that the intervention holds. The intervener's experience as a community developer or organization consultant gives that person a unique perspective from which to articulate this vision. In the early stages of an intervention, the stakeholders will be looking to the intervener for leadership and will give extra consideration to what he or she has to say about what they can accomplish through their collaboration.

The building of trust and openness in the change program starts with the intervener. He or she is the model (Figure 23) of authentic behavior–sharing joys and anxieties, and having consistent dealings with the stakeholders. Trust is based on authenticity and predictability. Risk taking is another essential component in all successful interventions and the intervener is the personification of this goal for stakeholders.

- TRUST
- CONSISTENT BEHAVIOR
- OPENNESS

- AUTHENTICITY
- PERSONAL LEARNING
- NEW WAYS OF DOING THINGS

Figure 23. The Intervener as a Role Model

A difficult decision for the intervener in giving leadership to the change program is choosing the appropriate role to take on controversial issues inside and outside the system. As an outsider the intervener may be able to stay aloof from these issues, citing a lack of knowledge. But as the role model of authentic, up-front, risk-taking communication, a carefully chosen, well-articulated position about issues is also a choice to consider. My bias is to stay out of the controversial issues unless I have the information and perspective to make a thoughtful response and unless I have sufficient energy and feelings about the issue to make withholding my opinion be not authentic for me.

Successful interventions are led by a person who also models a commitment to personal learning and development. This means predicting the likely outcomes of various actions, sharing uncertainties, and seeking feedback to determine the accuracy of the predictions. Like other risk-taking activities of the intervener, this is done very openly and the learning outcomes are frequently talked about with the stakeholders. This role model supports the stakeholders in taking similar risks and in being open about the positive and negative feedback that contributes to their learning and personal development.

Leadership Style

Our understandings at this time about leadership style (Dimock, 1987a) provide authoritative evidence that the intervener needs to be alert to balancing task-accomplishment behaviors with relationship and group-building behaviors. As the intervention gets started and the stakeholders are looking to the consultant for answers, a fairly directive style of leadership that provides a great deal of structure is most likely to be effective. As the intervention gets under way the challenge for the intervener is to increase supportive, group-building behaviors and to reduce structuring and giving direction. The primary method of empowering the stakeholders is giving them power. Decreasing direction and increasing support is the way this is done. Thus, by the action-taking phase of the intervention, the consultant should be giving a great deal of support and encouragement but only a small amount of direction. This change in leadership is difficult for many interveners and they either provide too little structure in the early stages or hang on too long in giving direction.

My position is that it is easier to withdraw direction than to add it. People who have been running their own shows resent too much direction and control over their activities. But they certainly appreciate being given more responsibility. In the early phases I recommend erring on the side of providing more direction; later in the intervention, based on sensitive consideration of the steering committee's competence and motivation, the intervener withdraws the direction slowly as soon as is feasible.

The intervener, then, consistently reduces direction and structuring activities in small bits, helping the group to take over each bit successfully. For example, he or she may chair the first meeting of the steering committee, providing structure and acting as gatekeeper to facilitate the participation of each member. Once the group is underway (after one to three meetings), the intervener would propose and structure the selection of a chairperson or perhaps an acting chair, or else obtain agreement to rotate the position among members. Hence, if the intervener were still in the chair by the goal-setting phase, I would assume that he or she were hanging on too long and creating dependency.

Proposing structure for the steering committee is a form of direction and control; yet it tells participants *how* to do something (process) rather than *what* decisions they should make (content). Direction is usually thought of as influencing or controlling what decisions will be made and who will do what to whom. Structuring interventions is a facilitative strategy that keeps the intervener in a consultant role rather than in the role of a high-control expert who tells members what to do. Structuring how to work at planning and implementing an intervention is the major contribution (and area of control) of the ICC intervener.

Recruiting and Building the Steering Committee/ Intervention Team

Many of the criteria for selecting steering committee members were reviewed when the committee was discussed in the entry phase of planning. Let me now review a few further considerations in recruitment and group building. The six most important factors in developing strong groups (Dimock, 1987a) are described in Figure 24.

---

1. Recruit members who will be attracted to the group.
2. Set clear and attainable goals.
3. Establish structures and rules to ensure the goals will be accomplished.
4. Encourage teamwork and the sharing of leadership.
5. Demand members invest significant time and energy in the group.
6. Make members aware of their personal contributions to the group's success.

Figure 24. Developing Strong Groups

The first consideration in selecting members, attraction to the group, consists in part of attraction to the vision of the intervention; however, at least as important is an attraction to the other members and the way they work together. The more members can meet their needs for recognition, approval, power, and new experiences in the group and the more they can feel empowered in the process, the greater will be their attraction to the group. Thus if the planning committee is seen as a high-status group that is going places and doing things, the recruitment of attracted members will be easy. Screening possible steering committee members using the criteria of how attractive they are likely to find the group is important in recruitment. This is an extension of the give/get technique. It is also possible that a source of attraction to the group is the intervener personally and/or professionally. In the participative style of the ICC method, most committee members will be approached by other committee members to be asked to join. However, the odd one may best be recruited by the intervener. This would likely be the case if the potential member were not well-known to the others, not in the same communication network, or perhaps a high-status person whom the others felt uncomfortable approaching.

The whole ICC method is built on the second and third considerations: setting clear and attainable goals and establishing structure to ensure their accomplishment. Encouraging teamwork and the sharing of leadership is also integral to the ICC method; yet two additional considerations are worth mentioning here. They are the unique skills and outside status of the intervener that enable him or her to facilitate internal networking perhaps better than anyone else. The intervener can invite two people in for coffee who might not otherwise talk to each other. He or she is the broker who can pull people together both internally and externally and encourage them to discuss mutual concerns. The intervener is well positioned to build coalitions and networks of potential supporters and collaborators. This increases teamwork both within the steering committee and with the rest of the community.

Being a member of the steering committee invariably takes a great deal of time and energy, and the trick of considerations five and six is to recognize and to feel proud about the amount of time spent in the committee and to take time to recognize each member's specific contributions. For example, after six or eight meetings the steering committee might take an hour and go around the group and give specific recognition to each member. For each person in turn, every other member would mention the contributions he or she has appreciated from that person. This individual recognition process can be further consolidated by capping it off with a total team recognition and celebration. A review of progress to date with a heavy focus on accomplishments is the method of celebrating small wins. When all of the members feel that they make a difference, that the committee is making good progress, that the work is exciting, and that they have a sense of belonging to this committee, they will be motivated, committed, and empowered.

Making Planning Meetings Effective

The expectation of a high level of task accomplishment is a powerful group builder. An important focus for team building is helping the committee to accomplish its tasks. A likely place for task accomplishment to be blocked is with ineffectively run steering committee meetings–or in the decision-making meetings of the stakeholder's group. Incompetence in facilitating decision making is also a common cause of a participative intervention's failure. Interveners and stakeholders end up frustrated; because they blame the collaborative method, they revert to the tried-and-true authoritarian approach, saying something like "you can't get all those people to make any decisions together."

At the point of setting priorities and making decisions for change, difficulties often arise. These are usually of a procedural nature as the decisions get hung up or conflicts flare. The participants experience considerable frustration and may react against the whole intervention and change process. Two techniques in group procedures that are most helpful here are a systematic problem-solving sequence and the avoidance of majority-rule decisions in favor of group consensus.

My preferred systematic problem-solving method is outlined in the Figure 25. A group's most likely area of difficulty in using the eight steps in sequence is separating suggesting solutions (4) from evaluating alternatives (5). Most groups want to start evaluating an idea as soon as they hear it. It takes a strong chairperson to hold them back until all of the possible solutions have been suggested.

Gaining and maintaining commitment from the participants is crucial to the ICC method of change; nowhere is it more likely to be neglected than at decision-making meetings. Decisions made by majority vote tend to polarize the group, reduce commitment, and possibly promote sabotage among those who lost the vote. It is more helpful to work toward consensus, in which everyone is encouraged to express his or her point of view, common ground is sought, and the group uses its cohesiveness and internal pressure to secure agreements that everyone can accept. Consensus does not mean holding out for total group agreement because one person's withholding agreement would have almost as much power as an autocrat.

Another place to work at increasing commitment is immediately after a decision is made. It is useful to encourage each person to express his or her feelings about the decision that has been made. If the group is still divided, it may help to set up a definite time in the future to review and perhaps reconsider the decision. Or, the use of the risk technique described in the next section may reduce resistance. In any case, the public expression of opinion about a decision increases the commitment of those who support it as well as those partly opposed.

The right-hand column of the Problem-Solving Guide (Figure 25) lists a number of possible methods to use at the different steps. Most of these methods have already been described, but let me

Problem-Solving Steps	Useful Member Roles	Blocks	Possible Methods
1. Defining the problem	Orienting Clarifying Defining problem	Ambiguity Different perceptions Generalizations	Problem census Small groups Needs analysis
2. Checking involvement	Testing Supporting Revealing interest	Silence "Yessing"	Going around the group Ranking priorities

3. Collecting information	Giving
	  information
	Orienting
	Summarizing
		Moving to next step
		  too quickly
		Lack of focus
			Force-field analysis
			Advanced
			  preparation
			Data collection

4. Suggesting solutions	Seeking opinions
	Giving opinions
	Coordinating
		Starting to
		  evaluate ideas
		Limited participation
		Minority not heard
			Brainstorming
			Small groups
			Nominal group
			  technique

5. Evaluating alternatives	Giving opinions
	Testing feasibility
	Mediating-
	  harmonizing
	Coordinating
		Emotional
		  distortions
		Conflicts
		Steamrolling
		Majority voting
		Loss of focus
			Guided discussion
			Going around
			Force-field analysis
			Role playing
			Risk technique

6. Decision making & gaining commitment	Giving opinions
	Coordinating
	Mediating-
	  harmonizing
	Testing for
	  consensus
		Majority voting
		Polarizing
		Uncommitted
		  going along
			Risk technique
			Provisional try
			Total group
			  discussion
			Protecting minority
			  opinions

7. Planning & implementation	Giving
	  information
	Testing feasibility
	Initiating
		Lack of involvement
		Generalizations
		Vague
		  responsibility
			Implementation
			  teams
			Small groups
			Committees

8. Evaluating & replanning	Coordinating
	Giving opinions
	Giving
	  information
		Expectations
		  not clear
		Implementation
		  mechanics not
		  clear
			Work groups
			Committee reports
			Data collection

Figure 25. Problem-Solving Guide

now round out the list. *Going Around* is a method whereby the chairperson says how important it is to hear each person's feelings about an issue. Each person in turn is then called on for any comments he or she chooses to share. This procedure quickly indicates where the group is and indicates the number of people supporting various views. Best of all, it facilitates the silent majority being heard and shifts the focus from the aggressive over-participators.

The *Risk Technique* is an extension of the force-field analysis that asks the participants to describe and to explore the possible risks involved in a specific course of action. The free expression of possible risks is encouraged in a brainstorming style in which no one can scoff at the reality of risk. This is important because many risks do not have any basis in fact or reality yet are effective blocks to action. Encouraging the expression of fears and then examining them in the light of day with support from others has proven to be highly effective in reducing these fears. And, as our assumption about change has stipulated, reducing the forces restraining a change is the best way to facilitate positive action.

Facilitating problem solving through *Role Playing* calls for a proposed solution to be acted out during a few minutes of the meeting to see more clearly what it might look like. For example, if someone had proposed that the best way to handle the lateness problem in the committee was to have private talks with the offenders, the chairperson/consultant would ask the person making the proposal to select another member of the group and imagine that that person had been late and actually show the meeting what would be said to the offender.

Training and Coaching Key Players

The intervener as organizer and leader of the change program is in an unique position to facilitate the training and coaching of the steering committee and other key players. There are likely new skills and new ways of working that are involved in building a strong steering committee and running effective planning meetings. The consultant may give direct leadership to some of these training activities or help mobilize community resources to do the training. In many interventions, I have designed and led group-building activities as the program got started and then trained and coached the committee in using the problem-solving guide and other skills in making meetings effective. As I am on many mailing lists, it is easy to describe the other training resources that are available and to help participants make contacts. And many steering committee members have ended up in my university courses and professional-development seminars. In fact, for many years I have made it a point to invite several key players of my current intervention programs to go along with me to the workshops and seminars I conduct; using them as program assistants gets them in for free as well as facilitates their training experiences.

The focus of the change program may be such that those people affected by it will be expected to do different things and they will look for help in developing the new attitudes and skills. Recently, a number of the change programs I have been working on resulted in human-service organizations deciding to shift their focus of service delivery from individuals to groups or the community. Once the stakeholders had agreed that this was the way to go, there was a clamor for training in group work or community-development skills. As a consultant with knowledge and experience in these areas, I was in a key position to either organize the training with the group myself or to help them to find competent resources in their internal or external community.

Thus, although increasing the personal and professional competence of those involved in the intervention program is not the primary focus of an ICC intervention (changing the social architecture or culture is), it is an inevitable part of all successful ones. It is not either a systems change or an adult-education situation. Learning and development are always part of the intervention; in the ICC model, training is one of the methods or supports for building new ways of doing things. As a trainer and supervisor of many hundreds of consultants, I have found training programs to be the most popular focus for entry and early stages of intervention activity. Given the competence of these new consultants in designing and conducting training programs, this seems quite appropriate.

It is clear that the intervener is a constant model of the attitudes and behaviors that the intervention is trying to promote. What is not as clear—and seldom discussed in books on community and organization development—is the intervener's role in coaching key players in the project. Sometimes the coaching is an extension of the intervener-as-model idea, in which the intervener draws attention to his or her actions and uses them as illustrations of an area of concern. Hence when the steering committee seeks direction on how it is going to introduce the intervention program to the nine departments in the organization, the consultant may say, "Well, one place to start might be taking a look at how I introduced the idea to you three weeks ago and exploring the strengths and weaknesses of how that approach worked out."

Informal coaching may take place between meetings, such as when the consultant gives feedback and encouragement during a coffee break by saying, "It was great to see you making that proposal about networking just now. I really hope you will follow up on it when we go back after coffee." Or when the frustrated chairperson says how difficult the meeting was to manage, the consultant may set up an informal coaching session by saying, "Let's get together an hour before the next meeting and look over your plans for it and maybe we can smooth out some of the trouble spots." Hopefully, this would provide an opportunity for the consultant to do some coaching on chairing-meeting skills, approaches to handling the over-participators, and increasing the structure to keep the meeting on the track. The two of them might even role play some of the difficult points the chair wants to make, and perhaps the consultant would model two or three ways that that point could be presented.

The person who is often under the greatest stress as an intervention starts taking hold is the head person of the community or organization. This person may be the senior elected official in a community, the unit head, or the chief executive officer (CEO) in an organization. I assume this person is heavily involved in the intervention and is likely on the steering committee but not necessarily the chair. It is difficult for the head person to have much of a support group within the organization, inasmuch as the top position tends to distance many people. The job at the top is frequently described as a lonely one as head people feel they have no one to confide in about their fears, concerns, and aspirations. Here is another important opportunity for the consultant to take on the role of coach.

Head people usually feel they have the most at risk in the intervention and therefore have fears that others do not share. They also may have the most to gain from the intervention; but as usual, fears dominate behavior. As we saw in discussing the *Risk Technique*, the free expression of fears in an accepting climate is a powerful method of reducing these fears. With these considerations in mind, I have been trying to increase my contact time with the head person in my interventions to build rapport and make myself available as a support system and coach. When I have done this well, it has been among the best uses of my time in the intervention. Usually I find it hard to think of myself as a major confidant, support person, and personal coach to this person who has tremendous power and earns ten times what I do; yet I am the interested, neutral outside person who has a lot of listening and helping skills. (This is getting easier because at least now I am usually older than they are and my financial assets often are greater.)

My suggestion to you as intervention leader is to make time early in the entry phase to sit down with the head person, to try to establish some rapport, and if things seem to be going well, to ask if the head person would be interested in discussing some of the possible strengths and weaknesses of the intervention. If the conversation moves in this direction, your authentic behavior would have you sharing your aspirations and fears about the possible intervention and encouraging and supporting sharing by the head person. At some point a question such as "What is the worst thing you think might happen in this intervention?" could help to focus on the risks and fears.

If the early rapport and sharing session seems helpful, the intervener could consider what time and frequency similar coaching sessions might warrant during the intervention. The intervener might play a useful role as a sounding board or continue with the coaching role in discussing how the intervention is going and what new risks or fears are emerging. The consultant is in a strategic position to give the head person descriptive feedback (especially if little is forthcoming from the group) and to encourage discussion of how the head person feels the consultant is working. Personal coaching could range from ways to be less defensive to how to manage conflict within the system.

As part of the "loneliness-at-the-top" syndrome, few system members have much awareness of the head person's personal thoughts and feelings of the pressures and concerns faced. They would in fact have a difficult time describing what life is like for their head person. As one of the intervention goals may be to increase this kind of communication and sharing, it is worth considering whether it would be productive to conduct one of the coaching sessions in front of the steering committee or intervention group. In these sessions of "let's try putting ourselves in the shoes of the head person and see how things look from that position," we carry on with our usual discussion of how things seem to be going. I ask those watching to withhold their comments or questions until the end, at which time we will process the whole session with the group. I structure the processing time to ensure it doesn't end up as a we/they bitch session with the group dumping on the head person and encourage the others to work as "assistant coaches."

The other key player in an intervention who may deserve special attention and coaching is the person who proposed or initiated the intervention, or the one whose job it is to "ride herd" over the intervention. As we discussed in the entry phase, many interventions start through a personal contact with someone in the system. For me this could be a former student, someone from one of my professional development or training programs, a friend, or a person who has read my books or articles. This person may be in charge of personnel or training or may just be a player in the system. The consideration is what special role, if any, this person should have in the intervention. If this person brought you into the system and supported you as a competent, helpful consultant, his or her reputation (and perhaps the job as well) is on the line. The risks this person is taking exceed those of other stakeholders. Sometimes it seems most appropriate to let this person off the hook by treating him or her in the same way as everyone else and not highlighting the initiating or managing role (the intervention may be paid for through this person's department budget so they sign all the checks). Often, though, it seems to me best to acknowledge this person's special role in the intervention and make him or her an assistant on the intervention team. This gives the person visibility and legitimacy in the intervention, likely increases status, and certainly expands the learning and training opportunities. When appropriate, I have included this person in my coaching sessions with the head person as both an inclusion and training activity but also in the hope the use of each other's resources would continue after I had departed.

Managing Conflict

The intervener also has a unique role in managing the conflict generated by the intervention. This role is related to the experience and skill of the consultant, the inside-and-outside the system status, the trust and respect earned, and the possibility that some stakeholders will see the consultant as responsible for what happens in the intervention. This is the last special area for the use of the consultant's organizing and leadership skills that I'll describe but it is not the least important. Dissatisfaction and conflict are the guts of any intervention–without them there would be no motivation to change the system.

The role of the intervener is to help the stakeholders learn how to harness and manage the tremendous energy that conflict produces and to use that tension to further the intervention goals. Most of us have mixed feelings about conflict and have ended up seeing some conflict as good and some as bad. On the hockey rink and the football field, conflict is good–without it there would be no game. But in the business organization and family, conflict is seen as bad even though it may still be an important dynamic of the "game" there. Management training teaches conflict-resolution skills as though the goal were to resolve conflicts and live happily ever after.

Interventions are, and should be, full of conflict–conflict over goals, conflict over values, conflict about how to do things (process), and conflict over power, status, and personalities. As intervention organizers, I advise we look at conflict as a neutral input and manage the conflict in ways that promote attitude and behavior change, that facilitate learning, and that produce results that enhance the program's goal achievement. I like the concept of *optimal tension*–enough to supply the juice for the change program but not so much that it immobilizes participants or develops warring factions.

Another source of conflict in an intervention is the conflict within the participants generated by the ambiguity of change program. When people don't know what is going to happen, what is going to be expected of them, and whether they will be adequate for the new order, tension is created. Ambiguity creates tension, and the tension plays out in the form of resistance and conflict.

A similar source of tension and conflict is from the ambiguity created by changing the system's social architecture–the usual roles, relationships, and pecking order. Even cows have an order in which they go through a gate and into the barn at milking time. Every cow's knowing her place in the order makes for an easy, peaceful entry into the barn. But add new cows or change barns, and the usual way of doing things has been upset. Now the cows jostle for position, shove, butt, and squeeze to all get through the door at the same time. This is constructive conflict; as soon as the cows work out a new gate order or resume the old one, the tension goes away and the activity runs smoothly. Group-building activities, especially those involving roles, status, and expectations, can be beneficial in managing this kind of conflict in an intervention.

Take the conflict out of most interventions and they would collapse. Yet interventions have failed because the tension level climbed too high and stakeholders hunkered down or fled to maintain their well-being. The task is to maintain an appropriate balance of anxiety-creating aspects of change with security-giving components (such as some structure and direction for the intervention, visibility of a competent and trusted consultant, and the support of a tight-knit group). This appropriate balance is called optimal tension. Sanctioning conflict and using it constructively helps to achieve optimal tension.

The consultant is the paramount role model in demonstrating a healthy openness to conflict. In a very visible way he or she can treat conflict as an everyday, expected occurrence and a source of motivation to get more involved and push on with the planning of change. Certainly it is not something to pretend is not happening or something to soothe over through immediate resolution. If the conflict is hidden or avoided by the group, the consultant can help to get it into the open. This may occur in a direct intervention naming the conflict, or by making process observations that focus on the problems the conflict is creating in the group. Or the intervener may share his or her personal feelings about the conflict and encourage others to do the same. Once the conflict is in the open the consultant can teach participants new ways to manage it.

The usual role of the intervener during a conflict is as a third-party consultant. The third-party role is one of neutrality on the issue, providing structure within which to explore the conflict, facilitating the process, problem solving ways to manage the conflict, analyzing or processing the experience, and consolidating possible learnings.

Power and control, as usual, are the principal focuses of conflict in an intervention. And one of the key players in that conflict is likely to be the consultant, whether he or she likes it or not. The intervener may see himself or herself bending over backwards to give power away and strengthen others. Yet as project organizer he or she has a lot of power to give away. It may also be valuable for the consultant to consider the track records of the key players and key subgroups in the project with regard to power and control. This would be like a stakeholder's analysis that asks how much power these individuals or subgroups have had and how much they want. The second question in the analysis is how much control these individuals and groups have accepted in the past and how much they are likely to accept now. Such an analysis may help to put the conflict over power into perspective and suggest some subsequent activities.

Part Eight

Personal Concerns of the Intervener

A major thesis of the Intervention and Collaborative Change model is the importance of the intervener as a person to the intervention's success. The following expectations for the intervener using this approach are high and demanding:

- Organizer;

- Role model;

- Leader;

- Coach and trainer;

- Resource for the ICC method and procedures; and

- Authentic person in the here and now.

Managing all of these roles while maintaining a balance with the outside world and the rest of your life is another of the challenges of an intervention. This challenge may well be one that determines the fate of a change program if the intervener becomes so emotionally involved and irretrievably enmeshed that he or she loses all perspective and allows the intervention to become his or her life. Interveners may also flee the hectic pace and conflict of an intervention by becoming remote and detached, losing their personal prestige and authenticity. It is a difficult balance to maintain; doing it well becomes very much a part of the consultant's total life style.

One dimension of the balance is pace–how many interventions can be worked on at the same time, how many hours a day can be put into an intervention, and what is happening in the rest of the intervener's life. Another challenge for the intervener is to find ways of meeting personal needs within or outside the intervention. It is important to have people to talk to about the hassles in an intervention and to get some personal support and recognition. Considering the usual hectic pace–the physical demands on a consultant–during the change project, it is a challenge to be physically capable of handling the expectations.

Personal Support System

The ICC process of systems change produces dynamics that usually include frustration and/or hostility directed toward the intervention. This hostility may be left over from previous interventions, may arise in a control phase if the intervener is perceived to have power, or may be the expression of resistance to change. If the intervener has mobilized a grass-roots group to coerce the system into certain actions, the hostility will be even more direct.

In a systems-change program it has been my experience that I rarely feel that I know all that is going on and am on top of it. This is in contrast to my work with individuals and small groups in which I usually feel on top of things. Systems change involves so many variables that a simple analysis and diagnosis of what is happening is very unlikely. This "not-knowing" feeling, coupled with an awareness that the intervention is not having much impact, has occasionally left me wondering about my competencies. I am also aware that I need a certain amount of positive reinforcement and social support as I work on an intervention.

As this became clearer to me a few years ago, I embarked on building an active support-system component into any intervention. I put a lot of energy, though a lesser amount of time, into the task of finding a person or group of people who would accept me and talk with me about what's going on or meet my needs in other ways. Immediately on moving into a new situation, I look around and start checking out where I am going to find my support. In some systems I build in a support system by creating a planning group or steering committee. In others I suggest a team which then has one or more of my colleagues working with me. Or I may take along students or key players from other projects to assist me. But in a lot of interventions I build my support system among the stakeholders: this usually does the trick and often leads to some permanent friendships.

The Social-Health Indicator of an Intervention (Figure 26) is to help you assess the strength of your social-support network in an intervention. If your answers to these questions average out to below the midpoint, the indicator suggests you should work at increasing your support and enjoyment or perhaps turn the intervention over to another consultant.

Health and Well-Being

Now that you have your personal support system in place or at least made its creation a priority, let's look at other factors contributing to your health and well-being. Eating, sleeping, fitness, and relaxation top the list here because interventions create special problems for all of them. Once the intervention begins, it is easy to get caught up in it and work late into the night, miss meals, settle for fast-food snacks, party with the participants after the day's work is done, and spend no time exercising or relaxing. These may seem like remote considerations while sitting in the comfort of your living room and reading this at your own pace, but interventions can be hectic, exciting beyond words, and entirely consuming.

On interventions away from home I have seen assistants and sometimes colleagues who could hardly stand up after a week in the field; if they sat down they tended to fall asleep. At one time I was working on three change programs each day, and after a few

Place an "X" on the line corresponding to your choice.

1. How much fun are you having in this intervention?

   None_____   Little_____   A bit_____   Lots_____

2. Is this intervention to *do* something or for something to do?

   Convenient job_____   So-so_____   Really important_____

3. How much approval, recognition, and satisfaction are you getting from this intervention?

   Little_____   Some_____   Fair bit_____   A lot_____

4. What is the norm for social support given by the steering committee (or the group where you spend the most time)?

   Little_____   Some_____   Fair bit_____   A lot_____.

5. How many stakeholders in the intervention do you talk to about our personal intervention concerns?

   None_____   1 or 2_____   2 or 3_____   4 or more_____

6. How many people outside this intervention do you talk to about concerns with this intervention?

   None_____   1 or 2_____   2 or 3_____   4 or more_____

7. While working on the intervention how often do you participate in a social, educational, recreational, church, or community group?

                                                     2 or more
   Rarely____ Once a month____ Once a week____ times a week____

8. Do you have a partner or spouse?

   No____   Sometimes____   A steady____   Married or live-in____

List your personal support-system people in this intervention

1._____   4._____

2._____   5._____

3._____   6._____

Figure 26. Social-Health Indicator of an Intervention

days I had difficulty remembering which group I was with and what their major issues were. Another colleague would get so tired that he would sleep in and miss the meetings with the group.

Over the years I have developed two practices that I think have helped me (and others who picked them up) deal with these forces. First is a *pacing* practice in which I think of the intervention as a marathon run; I spread out my energy to last the course. Part of my pacing includes getting a good night's sleep two nights out of three, eating one peaceful (non-working) meal a day, and getting in an exercise period at least every other day. The second practice to handle intervention pressures is taking charge of the planning for my personal well-being, especially when I am away from home. I plan or participate in the arrangements for travel, accommodations, food, working schedules, recreation, and opportunities for physical activity. The time I put into this is worth it ten times over, and my participation always saves the stakeholders money. Think and plan ahead about what will help to keep you in top form for your consulting challenges.

Personal and Professional Development

People are still arguing over whether leaders are made or born, but everyone agrees that outstanding leaders are all learners. Being a model of an adult learner for the stakeholders and helping then learn how to learn has been identified as a primary role of the consultant. Let's now look at intervener's learning and growth on a more personal focus again. This discussion was started early in this book when I talked about the personal qualities of the intervener. Many specific competencies and skills have been described as part of organizing the ICC program. Most of these were of a technical, procedural nature. Figure 27 brings us back to more personal qualities. Interveners rate themselves on this list as to their range on each item; they then use arrows to indicate the direction in which they would like to expand their range of behavior on that item. There are no best places to be on these items, but the direction of the

Place an "H" at the point of your highest level of behavior and an "L" at your lowest point. Select any areas you would like to work on further and draw an arrow showing the direction in which you would like your behavior to move.

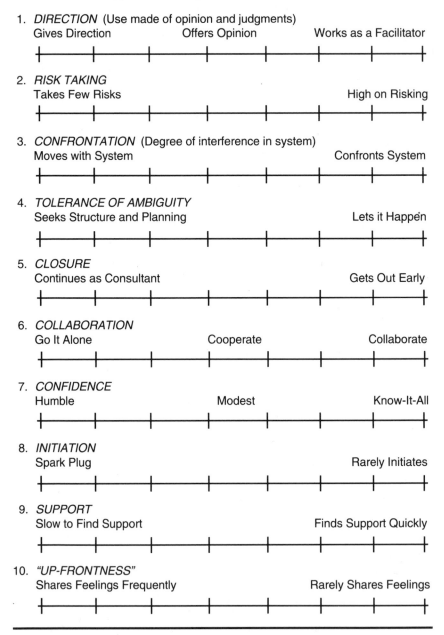

1. *DIRECTION* (Use made of opinion and judgments)
   Gives Direction   Offers Opinion   Works as a Facilitator

2. *RISK TAKING*
   Takes Few Risks   High on Risking

3. *CONFRONTATION* (Degree of interference in system)
   Moves with System   Confronts System

4. *TOLERANCE OF AMBIGUITY*
   Seeks Structure and Planning   Lets it Happen

5. *CLOSURE*
   Continues as Consultant   Gets Out Early

6. *COLLABORATION*
   Go It Alone   Cooperate   Collaborate

7. *CONFIDENCE*
   Humble   Modest   Know-It-All

8. *INITIATION*
   Spark Plug   Rarely Initiates

9. *SUPPORT*
   Slow to Find Support   Finds Support Quickly

10. *"UP-FRONTNESS"*
    Shares Feelings Frequently   Rarely Shares Feelings

Figure 27. Personal Considerations of the Intervener/Consultant

arrow shows your judgment of whether more or less of the quality would strengthen your competence. These items may help you focus on some of the goals for your personal learning.

Professional development and renewal are a must for the intervener as a part of keeping up to the cutting edges of the profession. Outside seminars, workshops, and courses also help interveners maintain perspective on their programs and usually provide new insights about what really happened.

Many consultants keep a professional journal (I call it a learning log) that helps them to think through what is happening in the change program and to be able to reflect on it later. It is a great way to assess an intervention. Related, focused reading is another important professional-development activity. And similar to the professional-journal experience, writing an article or case study about your experiences is another powerful way of enhancing your learning while hopefully contributing to the development of others.

Ethical Considerations

A specific, predetermined goal, such as a change in service delivery, does not need to be the goal of an intervention. The goal setting can be left to the system to determine after the intervention gets underway. This takes the intervener "off the hook" about the chief ethical concern of "who gets to do what to whom." Thus the intervener becomes a catalyst and just helps things that are already there to happen–the intervention becomes value free. Hiding behind some imagined neutrality (how many really neutral, value-free people do you know?) is not the style of the ICC approach in which the intervener is organizer, leader, and role model.

A current joke on consulting has it that the three biggest lies in society are: "It's in the mail"; "I'll respect you as much in the morning"; and "I'm from the government, I'm here to help you." Helping and intervening can just as easily be harmful as beneficial, yet many "helpers" talk about their work as if it were automatically good. I like the concept of intervention as it is clear you are interfering with the status quo, yet it is of neutral connotation keeping it clear that judgment of its helping or hindering is in the eye of the beholder or the evaluations of the stakeholders.

A number of years ago I was part of a team working on a community-development project with the Mistassini band of Cree Indians. Even then (and more so now with the James Bay Hydro Project I in place and Project II under consideration), it was critical to determine if the traditional aboriginal life style should be allowed to continue. Should the Crees be allowed, or possibly encouraged, to continue their hunting and fishing in remote family camps or should they be brought into the mainstream of contemporary Canadian life? The latter would mean compulsory education, government housing (most lived in tents), and jobs or welfare. What did helping them mean and who should decide what was helpful? Our team was split on this critical issue and we spent many a night discussing the ethical issues that were really our points of view.

Everything we do is an intervention in some way. Just getting up in the morning and breathing means we'll take good oxygen out of the air; if we turn on the lights and the coffee maker, we will consume non-renewable resources. To suggest that people don't have a right to intervene is nonsense. The real question is what are good (or honest) interventions.

It is unlikely that there are any universally good goals, and ones that seem self-evident in our society such as food, housing, health services, and education may take a back seat to more important political goals at any time. Let me propose the following three principles to speak to these questions about ethics:

1. People should have the freedom and opportunity to make informed choices about their lives.

2. The intervener is free to try to achieve personal-change objectives as long as these are clear to the social system and are negotiated with them.

3. The method of the intervention is of vital importance and the ends do not justify the means.

Free and informed choice suggests an exploration of the strengths and weaknesses of any choice along with a full consideration of other possibilities. It also implies a certain level of knowledge and awareness for the choice to be an informed one.

The second principle places a high value on the reciprocity of influence–the intervener may end up being more influenced by the social system than influencing it. A number of sociologists once went to a Billy Graham revival meeting to study his methods and ended up walking down the aisle to be saved. When every person is open and honest about his or her goals, it is a level playing field and the ball can go in any direction. Posturing a false goal (remember the "we're here to help you" joke) or withholding the goal leads to unethical manipulation.

The ends do not justify the means; in fact years after an intervention the goals are often forgotten but the activities are remembered. How many of us remember what the War of 1812 was about? But most of us know where the battles were fought and who won, and where forts and canals were built as a result of the war. Power and coercion help achieve goals but they are unlikely to leave the system more able to deal with change in the future.

This then is the question that penetrates to the core of these ethical concerns: "Is the system better off in its ability to deal with change in the future?" A system that has been manipulated, coerced, or brainwashed will not be better. Involvement, mutual negotiation, participation in decision making, and learning new group-building and problem-solving skills should help the system cope with future changing conditions in society. It is unlikely that an intervener's ethical philosophy determines his behavior as much as his desire for power and personal gain. If this is true the question to ask is: "Are you more interested in achieving your objective or leaving the system better able to manage future change?" This takes us back to the beginning of our intervention planning, which invovles being clear about our goals and motives in the intervention and deciding who is going to have what amount of control.

These then are the methods, skills, and personal qualities that are required for a successful ICC or any other participatory-change program. They represent high yet achievable competencies and help us to understand why so many well-meaning community and organizational-development programs based on stakeholder's participation have ended in frustration and dismay. Remember, there are no failures—only interventions that participants learn from and those they don't.

In selecting his generals, Napoleon was always told how competent they were; he would always ask, "But are they lucky?" Now that you have increased your competence—Good Luck!

Bibliography

Bavelas, A., & Strauss, G. (1961). Group dynamics and inter-group relations. In W.G. Bennis & others. (Eds.), *The planning of change*. New York: Holt, Rinehart & Winston.

Bennis, W.G., Beene, K., & Chin, R. (Eds.). (1985). *The planning of change*. New York: HBJ College Publications.

Block, P. (1981). *Flawless consulting*. San Diego, CA: University Associates.

Bryson, J.M. (1988). *Strategic planning for public and nonprofit organizations*. San Francisco: Jossey-Bass.

Dimock, H.G. (1978). The use of systems improvement research in developing change strategy for human service organizations. *Group and organization studies, 3* 365-375.

Dimock, H.G. (1979). Systems improvement strategies for community development. In D.A. Chekki (Ed.), *Community development: Theory and methods of planned change* (pp. 121-136). New Delhi, India: Vikas.

Dimock, H.G. (1987a). *Groups: Leadership and group development.* San Diego, CA: University Associates.

Dimock, H.G. (1987b). *A simplified guide to program evaluation.* Toronto: York University Campus, Captus Press.

Hersey, P., & Blanchard, K.H. (1988). *Management of organizational behavior.* Englewood Cliffs, NJ: Prentice-Hall.

Hornstein, H., & others. (Eds.). (1971). *Social intervention: A behavioral science approach.* New York: Free Press.

Lippitt, G., & Lippitt, R. (1986). *The consulting process in action.* San Diego, University Associates.

Peters, T.J., & Waterman, R.H. (1982). *In search of excellence: Lessons from America's best-run companies.* New York: Harper & Row.

Sarason, S.B. (1967). Towards a psychology of change and innovation. *American Psychologist, 23,* 227-233.

Schein, E.H. (1985). *Organizational culture and leadership.* San Francisco: Jossey-Bass.

Schein, E.H. (1988). *Process consultation: Vol. II. Lessons for managers and consultants.* Reading, MA: Addison-Wesley.

Sorenson, R., & Dimock, H.G. (1955). *Designing education in values.* New York: Associated Press.

Resources

Resource A
ORGANIZATION-SCAN GUIDE

CLIMATE

Emotional Climate

- Open/Closed? Directive/Participative? Trust/Suspicion? Repressive/Developmental? Company-oriented/Worker-oriented? Cooperative/Competitive? Morale and satisfaction level?

- Ways of working generally accepted or resisted?

- Personal sharing and self-disclosure? Supportive? Accepting? Judgmental? Critical? Secure? Anxious? Sources of support?

- Public expression of fears, desires, concerns?

Physical Climate

- Lighting? Ventilation? Layout of equipment? Colors? Use of space?

- Patterns established by physical setup?

- Messages of work environment?

INVOLVEMENT

- What motivates members to stay in the system? To leave?

- What makes system attractive? Rewards? Punishments?

- How much stake in outcomes?

- Informal structure and norms?

- Responsibility felt for system goals? Absenteeism? Turnover? Lateness?

- Areas of involvement (other available opportunities)? Level of involvement?

INTERACTION

- Who has what power?

- Lines of communication? Direction? Flow?

- Timeliness and accuracy? Reception? Status of units?

- Status hierarchy? Position power? Prestige power? Subgroup or cliques?

- Interaction between units? Job-oriented? Person-oriented?

- Role of formal/informal leaders or supervisors? Formal system vs. informal?

- Factors affecting interaction (shifts, location of units, common meals)?

- How is conflict handled? Sex roles?

COHESION

- Level of cohesion?

- Strength of pressures to conform to system norms? Extent of conformity/deviation? Form of pressures?

- Subgroup or unit differences in solidarity? Acceptance of nonconformists?

- Clarity and strength of values?

PRODUCTIVITY

- Clarity of goals?

- Source of goals? Internal/external? Degree to which goals are shared?

- Where and how are major decisions made? Effectiveness of decision-making structures?

- Evaluation and feedback of internal/external needs? How is productivity assessed (feedback and use by system)?

- Budget allocations related to organization priorities?

- Clarity of roles and functions? Duplication or overlapping?

- Flexibility of procedures? Extent of experimenting with new procedures?

Resource B
COMMUNITY-SCAN GUIDE[1]

History and Culture

1. "Official" history.

2. Informal culture—traditions, folklore, values—"the usual ways of doing things" [See Figures 13 & 14].

Physical Environment

1. Geographical layout, physical features [transportation, structures, etc.].

2. Population distribution [what groups live where, density, resources].

3. Out-of-area interaction [trade, recreation, work, government] and relationships [family, friends, church].

4. Climate [impact on community life and activities such as farming and recreation].

Resources

1. People—demographic data. Current issues related to race, religion, age, ethnic group, sex roles and orientation, etc.

2. Technology—transportation, administration, communication, financial, equipment, industry.

3. Natural—land, water, forests, minerals, energy sources.

---

[1] I offer my appreciation to Des Connor for stimulating this guide and helping with its content.

4. Capital. Where are financial resources? Internal/external? [Taxes, government resources, fund raising].

Power and Control

1. Which individuals have power? Who controls whom and how? [See Figure 8].
2. Which groups have power?
3. Leadership patterns presently in play?
4. Potential leadership for this ICC project?
5. Who "votes" or influences the decision-making process?
6. Role of government?
7. Patronage and "rules of the game" to get things done here?
8. Influence of family, schools, church, media, social agencies?

Education

1. Literacy and schooling, technical and professional?
2. Formal and informal educational resources?
3. Values, norms, goals, and methods of educations system? How adequate and current is the system for community needs?
4. Who's involved?

Religion

1. Who's involved in what formal or informal groups or organizations?
2. Culture, values, norms [usual practices of religious or spiritual groups]? Impact on community?
3. Resources and activities/programs of major groups?

Health and Welfare

1. Services, technology, and personnel available?

2. Norms and enforcement regarding health regulations?

3. Use [Who uses these services? Access? Convenience?].

Recreation

1. Who's involved in what—informal or organized?

2. Recreation resources [buildings, equipment, personnel, associations, leagues, links with other communities?].

3. Impact on community especially physical health and well-being.

Community Groups

Information about other groups not included under preceding categories, such as business, political, community-service, ethnic, or special-interest groups.

General Concerns

Likely overall attitude to proposed intervention? To internal/external consultant? Likely success based on previous patterns?

Resource C
THE TEN MOST WIDELY USED AIDS
TO DECISION MAKING

1. *STRAW VOTING:* Participants are asked to vote to give a general impression of reactions, not to make a decision. If there are several alternatives, I usually give each participant three votes to get a broader picture of reactions.

2. *NEGATIVE VOTING:* Participants are asked to identify alternatives they favor the least or could not accept.

3. *RANKING ALTERNATIVE:* Participants are asked to rank order the alternatives from the most favorable to the least favorable. The most favorable is assigned a "1" and the total of the number of alternatives is the least favorable. The totals or average ranks are presented to the group for further work.

4. *WEIGHTING ALTERNATIVES:* Similar to rank ordering but participants are given five or ten weights to assign to the various alternatives. The weights can be assigned in any way from all on one item to equal distribution.

5. *PRO/CON TECHNIQUE:* Participants make up two lists on a flip chart, one showing all the favorable factors and the other showing all the unfavorable factors of a specific issue or plan. This clarifies all the reasons the proposal may not work and surfaces the fears restraining a decision.

6. *CRITERIA MATRIX:* Criteria for evaluating the proposals are listed before the proposals are generated. After the proposals are summarized and reduced to a working number, they are assessed or scored according to the predetermined criteria and the results compared.

7. *GOING AROUND THE GROUP:* The facilitator goes around the group asking each person in turn what he or she thinks about a specific issue. A polarized discussion that gets bogged down may be freed up by hearing from the silent majority.

8. *ACTIVE-LISTENING DISCUSSION:* Each member is asked to summarize the last speaker's point of view—and to check the summary with that person—before he or she can express an opinion. When sensitive issues become polarized, listening often ceases as participants spend the time while others are talking preparing their next comment.

9. *TRIALS-WITH-EXPERIENCE REPORTS:* When two to four alternatives seem equally useful, they are tried out on an experimental basis for a specific period of time and then reported back on to give the group more data on the possibilities. And it may turn out that there is more than one successful way of handling the situation.

10. *CONFIDENTIAL LISTING OF OPINIONS:* Opinions or votes on a critical issue are collected and presented anonymously; this often diffuses much of the emotion and confrontation of a verbal discussion. The Delphi Technique and Nominal Group Technique use this strategy by asking members to give opinions in writing and then summarizing the responses for further work.

Resource D
THE TEN BEST WAYS TO IMPROVE MEETING EFFECTIVENESS

1. Establish clear and attainable goals.

2. Set up the procedures and structures to make sure they are accomplished.

3. Use the Dimock Group-Roles Method (or the Interaction Method) to share the leadership and use the group's resources.

4. Follow the logical steps in a problem-solving format.

5. Use brainstorming to generate creative suggestions (and avoid discussion of their weaknesses and strengths at that time).

6. Form subgroups to increase contributions and decrease interpersonal dynamics (reports are made on behalf of the subgroup).

7. Do regular process analysis—especially when the group is stuck or winding down (surfacing hidden agendas, power plays, deviations from agreed-on procedures, and unresolved conflict).

8. Have the group contribute to the meeting's agenda, which is circulated in advance of the meeting.

9. Work toward general agreements on decisions and be prepared to establish task forces to try out more than one favorable alternative (avoid win/lose majority voting).

10. Establish time lines and responsibilities for all decisions/action plans and update the progress on the relevant tasks at every meeting.

Resource E
CHECKLIST FOR ASSESSING AN
INTERVENTION PLAN

(To be completed by the steering committee.)

Rating Key: 1 = Needs more attention or isn't clear
2 = Seems O.K.
3 = Plans well in place

Area	Comments	Rating
1. Clarity of overall goals for intervention		
2. Identification of target system and its members		
3. Organogram and analysis of power in the system.		
4. Clarity of timetable, financial, personnel, and other resources.		
5. Description of credibility-building plans.		
6. Experience with previous interventions considered.		
7. Description of strategy (directing, persuading, problem solving).		
8. Role of intervener—amount of control expected.		
9. Force-field analysis of factors related to plans.		
10. Proposals made to reduce restraining forces.		
11. Description of the norms the intervention is expected to change.		

Area	Comments	Rating
12. Description of method for gaining acceptance of plans.		
13. Procedures for involving those affected by the change.		
14. Methods proposed for gaining acceptance of plans.		
15. Clarification of leverage points the intervention will use.		
16. Data collection on needs (tools and collection methods).		
17. Assessment of present group functioning.		
18. Data-analysis procedures (methods and by whom).		
19. Who sets goals? Using what procedures?		
20. Acceptance-gaining procedures for action plans.		
21. Consideration of impact of change on related systems.		
22. Training of participants in use of planned-change methods.		
23. Follow-up and action-stabilizing plans.		
24. Description of next round or closure procedures.		
25. Disengagement of consultant/intervener.		
26. Evaluation design (tools and collection methods).		
27. Report and replanning procedures.		
28. Reports or other documentation of intervention.		
29. Overall intervention closure.		

◆ Editor:
   Marian K. Prokop
Cover Design:
   Susan Odelson
Interior Design, Art, and Page Composition:
   Judy Whalen
Editorial Assistance:
   Linda McMakin

This book was edited and formatted using 486 PC platforms with 8MB RAM and high resolution, dual-page monitors. The copy was produced using WordPerfect software; pages were composed with Ventura Publisher software; cover and art were produced with CorelDRAW software. The text is set in thirteen on fifiteen Goudy Old Style, and the heads are set in Panache Bold. Proof copies were printed on a 400-dpi laser printer and final camera-ready output on a 1200-dpi laser imagesetter by Pfeiffer & Company.